D1409788

"Almost invariably the 'you' to whom the Lord addresses his words in the New Testament is plural, hidden in our ambiguous English form for the second person, but clearly directed at a community of disciples as such.

"Building on that reality, Cleary has compiled a book of prayers for parish groups. His images are gathered from the psalms and paraphrased at times to render their native crispness more intelligible. They are interwoven with the realities of our everyday lives to make them perfect starters for the meetings we frequent in every parish. Tolerance, forgiveness, and even the silence of God or the acceptance of God's surprises are celebrated in these services.

"I recommend this volume for the use of any parish minister or council member. The psalms will come alive in a new way."

Most Reverend Richard J. Sklba
Auxiliary Bishop of Milwaukee

"*Psalm Services* is a wonderful reincarnation of one of the pillars of Judaeo-Christian spirituality. All of the phases of faith and feeling are here, with modern as well as ancient nuances. The inclusive language and theology make this resource exceptionally useful in ecumenical settings."

Madonna Kolbenschlag
Author, *Kiss Sleeping Beauty Good-Bye*
and *Lost in the Land of Oz*

"Certainly *Psalm Services* is not only for parish gatherings. Try them in some of the informal neighborhood groups that might gather to discuss politics or any grassroots action on social and environmental problems. These services—short, lively, reverent, and in touch with the world we live in—are ideal for gathering, focusing, and motivating the kind of base communities out of which all sound liberation theology must flow."

Quentin Quesnell
Roe/Straut Professor in the Humanities
Smith College

PSALM SERVICES FOR GROUP PRAYER

WILLIAM CLEARY

XXIII

TWENTY-THIRD PUBLICATIONS

Mystic, Connecticut 06355

Illustrations by William Baker

Twenty-Third Publications
185 Willow Street
P.O. Box 180
Mystic CT 06355
(203) 536-2611
800-321-0411

ISBN 0-89622-526-7
Library of Congress Catalog Card Number 92-81718

DEDICATION

This effort is dedicated
to my dear musical sons Tom and Neil
each of them a holy book about the divine.
May all their songs
be psalms.

Contents

Psalm Services
for Group Prayer

Introduction: Why Pray?

This book of Psalm Services is designed to either jump-start new prayer groups, or open established groups to something fresh and new. The eighteen psalms from the Bible—newly paraphrased—should have a fresh feel to them, and the eighteen original psalms attempt an updated and modern flair. A touch of music is added as a challenge, if anyone is feeling venturesome.

For more than ten years, a small prayer group I belong to has met several times a month. Recently, after our prayers, our questioning and conversation centered on prayer itself. Afterwards, I hurried home and tried to remember the unusual dialog we had had. It speaks of many aspects of prayer—as this book attempts to do also.

The discussion started off when one person said, "I visited my shoemaker today and he told me that his daughter had a terrible accident some time ago. He claimed that her life was saved by a network of people praying for her. I can't imagine how that could be true. God could not save Holocaust victims where thousands died daily for years amid a maelstrom of prayers to God to stop it."

A young mother and physical therapist member of the group said, "I am also not comfortable praying for miracles. Praying for miracles—to save you from injuries in an accident or healing of a disease—would show, really, a *lack* of faith rather than showing faith. You might be feeling a lack of faith in God's way in the world (where evil has so much power), and a lack of confidence in God's total compassion and sympathy and empathy for us all. To ask God to 'have mercy,' for instance, might actually be objectively offensive to God—since God *is* mercy, and is infinitely merciful, even without petitions for it from creatures. Everything about God is mercy. One doesn't ask a kindly parent to 'have mercy.' The parent might be justifiably offended."

A college professor of religion replied, "But I know I would instantly cry out to God somehow if one of my loved ones were hurt or in terrible danger."

A store manager somewhat agreed: "Could it be," he asked, "that we just have no better language for talking to God but the human language we know—so that words like 'God, please have mercy on my daughter' really is crying out with the best words we have—which admittedly are inadequate?"

Then a psychologist in the group changed the direction of the conversation just a bit. "I think the Philokalia style of prayer is best for me: in the presence of God, to hold the person *in your mind in your heart.*"

"I can't disagree with that," said the physical therapist, "but what's most important, I think, is just to give time to reflection. That's what I call prayer. For me, quiet thought is always in the presence of God. At those times, God draws the prayers out of us."

There was a thoughtful silence for awhile. Finally someone said: "Yes, and could we think of it this way: the human ideal is to have communities everywhere *where each person is in the heart of every other person*—a community of love—so that especially in trouble, pain, loss or fear, everyone in the community would be sharing in everyone else's life, holding them in their mind in their heart—before God?"

A man who is a high school religion teacher added his thoughts. "That helps explain the strength and purpose of intimate groups like this where we open our hearts to each other. That way we can all share in the riches of the joys and concerns of the others, since joy is multiplied when it's shared, and concern and sorrow become more bearable when others bear it with you."

Someone then brought us back to the original question. "I wonder if such 'communal caring' might have great power somehow, either just some kind of ESP-type of communication of power to heal, or else some psychological effect on a person's psyche and spirit and mind, to know that many people are thinking about you, praying for you, holding you in their heart before God. That itself might be healing."

Our musician member then said, "Like the case of a little boy I know who was in terrible pain, shortly after he had been struck by a car, and the doctors did not want to give him anasthetics that might disguise the symptoms. His parents were at his hospital bedside, and his mother began to sing childhood songs to him—and the father noticed immediately that the heartbeat meter registered that the child's heart was slowing down, showing that the child was feeling comfort, feeling better, feeling positive, losing his fears. When the song was over, the father noticed that the heartbeat meter went back up. So the parents tried another song. The meter slowed down again. And so those parents stayed in the hospital throughout the whole night—singing. The vibes of their caring was healing the pain. The music was the best medicine!"

A social worker in the group spoke up and said, "Perhaps one prayer ideal, then, might be thought of as 'making harmonies' out of life, where each member of the common circle, by holding each other person in their heart, is contributing their own unique note or melodious sound to the common chord, making an ever richer kind of music vibrating outward—and inward—from that circle."

The psychologist added, "And just as every musical chord can always use another high note or low note or a sound of a new timbre or color, so the wider the circle of people who pray and feel together, the more beautiful the chord."

A bookkeeper participant then said, "Maybe that shoemaker's friends who prayed for his injured daughter created an almost irresistable harmony, which had its effect even far away, and overcame whatever injuries there were and set the self-healing into motion very strongly. I have heard many mysterious healings described as a quickening of the self-healing process."

Then the high school religion teacher said, "I wonder if that might explain the "power" of the prayer of petition: that it is often an act of solidarity with others who are praying—and in itself a powerful and effective communal human act."

We closed when someone summed it up this way: "Maybe lots of prayer, or one very good kind, is simply reflectiveness and *yearning*." And there seemed to be general agreement on that.

Psalm Services For Group Prayer would have been impossible without my community with these dear friends over many years. In the circle with them, it has been a rich and close harmony indeed.

William Cleary

Lovely Is Your Dwelling Place
from Psalm 84

CALL TO WORSHIP

Leader   May the Spirit of God be with you.

All   And also with you.

Leader   Receive our prayer today, Guiding God, as a harmony of hearts. Together we are before you, each of us with a unique voice, a unique story, a distinctive background, a distinctive future—but at this moment, behold us as a single circle, turned toward you. Teach us, together, to pray.

All   Blest be God forever.

ANTIPHONAL PSALM
(Group A—or Leader—reads **bold** *lines. The others read regular lines.*

Lovely is your dwelling place, O God of multitudes
     My soul longs for your presence
     My heart and soul sing out to the living God

     The sparrow finds a dwelling
          and the swallow builds a nest
               where she may lay her young:
               even your sacred altars, O God of multitudes
   Blest are all who dwell in your house
          ever singing your praises

O God of Reality, hear our prayer
     and listen to our hearts that turn to you
Behold, you are our shield
     look now with joy upon the faces of your anointed ones

     One day in your house is better than a thousand elsewhere
          I would rather be a doorkeeper in the house of my God
               than dwell in royal tents of wickedness
     For our God is a sun and a shield
          and honors us with grace and blessing

O God of multitudes
forever blest are all who trust in you

RELATED GOSPEL READING
Matthew 5:1-12 In his mountainside sermon, Jesus teaches about blessedness.

SILENT MEDITATION

Leader   For a few minutes in silence, ask for the gift of "a heart skilled in listening." Consider the words of the psalm and of our Gospel reading. *(After a period of silence, the Leader goes on.)*

JOYS AND CONCERNS

Leader   Each of us have a lifetime of joys and concerns in our hearts. Let us open our hearts just a little to one another, broadening everyone's prayers, and believing that what happens to us is important for the coming reign of God. *(Pause.)*

GROUP PRAYER

Leader   Our first prayer is for the gift of prayer itself. Holy Spirit, hear our prayers as we may improvise them now; or hear our silence for that too is our prayer. *(Any who wish may add their prayer.)*

CONCLUDING PRAYERS

Leader   Holy God, Creator of the Universe, Source of all life, and Healer of all wounds, receive these prayers of ours in harmony with the prayers and silences of all of creation. Grant that our hearts may expand to include the prayers of others, and that we may join in the circle of all who give you worship, trust, and love.

All   Blest be God forever.

Leader   Glory be to the Creator and to the Christ and to the Holy Spirit.

All   As it was in the beginning, is now, and ever shall be, world without end. Amen.

Life-Giving Mystery
Psalm of Awe

CALL TO WORSHIP

Leader   May the Spirit of God and of our Lord Jesus Christ be with you.

All   And also with you.

Leader   Holy Spirit of God, lead us in prayer. We know not how to pray, but believe that you speak to us in real events. We listen for your word.

All   Amen.

ANTIPHONAL PSALM
*(Group A—or Leader—reads **bold** print. The others read regular print.)*

Life-giving Mystery, Source of our life
we know that even when a human being is not "performing"
>**playing a Chopin prelude like lightning on the piano**
>**or twisting through a spectacular high dive into a pool**
>**or discovering in a microscope a cure for small pox**

even when a human being is sitting still in a chair
>**many indescribable wonders are happening**
>We praise your wonders, Spirit, loving, freeing,
>In you we live and move and have our being.

My heart beats away quietly in my chest, and I hardly feel it
>**unable to attend to the muscular drama there**
>>**many times a minute**

>**as blood is sent cascading through my lungs**
>>**collecting what nourishes cells**
>>**exchanging needs with plant life as I breathe**
>Life-giving Spirit, loving, knowing, freeing,
>In you we live and move and have our being.

My impulse to breathe comes gratuitously from you
>**Divine Source of Life and Wonder**

as does my impusle to eat and drink
>**but in secret my body processes the nourishment**
>>**and in secret my pulsing blood carries it to each cell**
>**where each tiniest atom**
>**throbbing with almost infinite complexities**
>>**carries out its beautiful task: my life. . .**
>We praise you, God, creating, loving, freeing,
>In you we live and move and have our being.

6

Almost without notice, I grow and move and feel
as my astonishing brain monitors all its connections
to every part of my body
And behold! I can hear, I can see
I can smell and taste and feel
and think, and remember
and somehow even love and care and desire
and build bridges of eternal relationship
to dozens of other humans
I can hope, thinking of an expanding future
and even believe in a world
beyond all I know through my senses
We praise you, Spirit, loving, knowing, freeing,
In you we live and move and have our being.
Even sitting still in a chair, I am surrounded by wonders within me
and outside me: this orbiting earth
circling a fiery star
swirling rhythmically within its galaxy of other stars
all amid the unimaginable cosmos of endless distances
I give thanks to be a part of it all
and most of all, to know my God is Love
We praise your wonders, Spirit, loving, freeing,
In you we live and move and have our being.

RELATED GOSPEL READING
Mark 1:12-13 Jesus spends forty days of prayer in the desert.

GROUP PRAYER

Leader We ask, Holy Spirit, for the gift of prayer, that we may find words to express our needs, hopes, and gratitude. Hear our prayers and our silence. *(Pause for prayers.)*

CONCLUDING PRAYERS

Leader Let us go in peace, blessed with an awareness of God's care for us, bringing in our hearts the prayer that we may always be reverent toward the mystery of our being, and grateful for the community of the church.

All Blest be God forever.

Leader Glory be to the Creator and to the Christ and to the Holy Spirit.

All As it was in the beginning, is now, and ever shall be, world without end. Amen.

Center of the Universe
Psalm in Silence

CALL TO WORSHIP

Leader   May the God who loves justice be with you.

All   And also with you.

Leader   Let us pray this psalm in the silence of our hearts. (*If all do not have a copy, the Leader says: "We open our hearts to this meditation before the face of God present among us and within us." Then the Leader reads it.*)

Spirit of God
I am not the center of reality, the center of the universe,
> **the midpoint around which existence circles**
> **even though my prayers often begin with that illusion**

I am more a needle on the spruce tree
> **a puff of mist in the middle of a dome of clouds**
> **a migrating Canadian goose eleventh from the end of the Vee**

It's just a little humorous
> **how individualistic I can become**
> **how fixed on myself as I try to relate to you**

Six billion of us look to you
> **for our daily nourishment of bread and community**
> **and that's just this billionith part of the Milky Way**
>> **which is itself a millionith part of the cosmos**
>>> **which is all we know of the still much larger reality**

I am not its center
> **you are**

And you stand under all that is
you give everything its being and its meaning and its destiny
And your exploding creation surrounds you
> **with adoration and dependence,**
> **with speechless awe and a few inadequate words—like these**

Isn't it a comical hallucination
> **that you seem to look straight at me and hear my prayer**
> **residing, as you listen, somehow in front of me and above me**
> **instead of under me and all around me**
> **and within me and all through me—which is closer to the truth?**

I know I need to say nothing
> **that if you wanted eloquent prayers from me**
>> **you would gift me with eloquence**

8

Accept instead my smile of illumination and relief
 and my surrender to all that is
  hanging here photosynthicizing on my blue spruce mother
  sweeping along with my misty ocean companions
   in the sky
  flapping through the air-crease passed on
   by Number Twelfth-from-the-End Goose
 grateful to be a part of it at all
 without the responsibilities of being its center

RELATED GOSPEL READING
Matthew 6:25-33 Jesus teaches how to put an end to some anxieties.

SILENT MEDITATION

Leader Let us give a few minutes to silent meditation, calling silently on God to speak to our hearts. *(After a period of silence, the Leader goes on.)*

JOYS AND CONCERNS

Leader Holy Spirit, see into our hearts, to all our concerns, worries, disappointments, and bewilderment; as well as to all our joys and reasons for gratitude. In the words of those who care to share their joys and concerns with us, hear also the silent prayers of all of us. *(Pause.)*

GROUP PRAYER

Leader Hear our prayers, Gracious Spirit, as we improvise them now—or listen to the silent prayers of our hearts. *(Pause for prayers.)*

CONCLUDING PRAYERS

Leader Holy Center of all that is, we give you thanks that we can learn from our mistakes and laugh at our own childishness. With you at our side, around us and within us, we firmly believe that we can learn to live without illusions, yet full of faith in your unseen world, in solidarity with our companions on the way, and in union with the Cosmic Christ, who works within us to bring about your reign on earth.

All Blest be God forever.

Leader Glory be to the Creator and to the Christ and to the Holy Spirit.

All As it was in the beginning, is now and ever shall be, world without end. Amen.

God Put a Song in My Mouth
from Psalm 40

CALL TO WORSHIP

Leader May the Spirit of God be with you.

All And also with you.

Leader Look upon us, Creating God, and create among us a community of prayer, speaking as one in a circle of friends, before you in reverence and humility, honored to be among those you have chosen to exist, and respectful of all the others in this circle and in our human race.

All Blest be God forever.

ANTIPHONAL PSALM
*(Group A—or Leader—reads **bold** lines. The others read regular lines.)*

God put a new song into my mouth
> **a song of praise to our Creator**
Many will hear and feel wonder
> **and put their trust in God**
> Blessed is the one who trusts in the Spirit
> who does not depend on the proud
> nor go astray after gods that are false
You have multiplied, my God
> **your wondrous deeds and generous thoughts toward us**
> **none can compare with you**
Were I to proclaim and tell of them
> **they would be beyond numbering**
> Still, sacrifice and offering is *not* what you desire
> > but you have given me instead a heart skilled in listening
> Burnt gifts and sin offerings you have not required.
> Then I said, Behold, I come!
> > In the front of the book it is written of me:
> > > My God, your will is my joy
> > > Your law is inscribed on my heart.
I have told the glad news of our rescue
> **in the hall of the great congregation**
Behold, I have not restrained my lips
> **as you well know, O my God.**
> I have not kept secret your saving help
> I have spoken to all of your mercy

I have not concealed your steadfast love
and your faithfulness to the covenant
Do not, then, O God, withhold your mercy from me your faithful servant
Let your steadfast love and your faithfulness ever keep me safe
For evils without number have encircled me
My troubles surround me till I hardly can see
They are more numerous than the hairs of my head
My heart almost fails in my anguish
For behold, I am poor, I am needy
but the God I trust takes thought for me
You are my help and deliverer
do not tarry, my God and my Hope

RELATED GOSPEL READING
Matthew 9:9-13 Jesus explains his own calling.

SILENT MEDITATION

Leader   In silent meditation let us each approach God who is greater than our hearts. *(After a period of silence, the Leader goes on.)*

JOYS AND CONCERNS

Leader   Now let us take a few minutes to consider our own joys, sorrows, and appreciations, and to share them with the group if we wish. Thus we enable all to be in solidarity. *(Pause for joys and concerns.)*

GROUP PRAYER

Leader   Give us, Divine Spirit, the gift of prayer, so that our hearts may rise to praise and confidence in you. Enrich our communal life and mutual understanding and acceptance. *(Pause for improvised prayers.)*

CONCLUDING PRAYERS

Leader   Faithful God, hear our prayers of gratitude for your goodness to each of us all our lives long. Our hearts sing of your goodness and kindness to us, and we give thanks that your promise is to be with us forever.

All   Blest be God forever.

Leader   Glory be to the Creator and to the Christ and to the Holy Spirit.

All   As it was in the beginning, is now, and ever shall be, world without end. Amen.

O God, You Are My God
from Psalm 63

CALL TO WORSHIP

Leader   May the Spirit of God be with you.

All   And also with you.

Leader   Give each of us, Holy Mysterious Spirit, an inner calm and quiet, so that we may learn to respond to your grace as you lead us to prayer and inspire in us "unutterable groanings." We turn to you together today in the belief that where two or three are gathered in the name of Jesus, he is in our midst, living in us and guiding us in all our prayers and desires.

All   Blest be the name of God.

ANTIPHONAL PSALM
*(Group A—or Leader—reads **bold** lines. The others read regular lines.)*

O God, you are my God, I seek everywhere for you
    my soul longs for you
    my body thirsts for you
        as in a dry and thirsty desert without water

I have seen your beauty in the holy place
    beholding your strength and your radiance
Because your steadfast love is better than life
    my lips will praise you always

So I will bless you as long as I live
    I will lift up my hands and call on your name

When I think of you upon my bed
    and meditate on you in the watches of the night
        my soul is feasted as with delicious pleasures
        and my mouth praises you with joyful lips
            for you have been my help
            and in the shadow of your wings I sing

So I will bless you as long as I live
    I will lift up my hands and call on your name.

RELATED GOSPEL READING
Matthew 10:24-33 Jesus warns his disciples of their travails to come.

SILENT MEDITATION

Leader   In the silence of our hearts, let us open the door of our being to the entrance of the mystery of God. *(After a period of silence, the Leader goes on.)*

JOYS AND CONCERNS

Leader   We struggle, Divine Creator, to believe in ourselves, to believe that all our joys and concerns are important to you, and can be important to one another. If any in the group care to speak of particular blessings or needs, now is that time. *(Pause for joys and concerns.)*

GROUP PRAYER

Leader   Holy Spirit, hear our prayers as we improvise them now, either aloud or in the silence of our hearts—for that too is prayer. *(Pause for prayers.)*

CONCLUDING PRAYERS

Leader   We have fears, O God of the Universe, as you see plainly in our hearts. And we have hopes, as you know. And we have faith, our faith in you. Strengthen us today, then, against all the challenges and disappointments ahead, and prepare us to receive in endless gratitude your salvation in the end. For we proceed in the dark but we believe in the light, and we bear with our ignorance and egotism without ever despairing of your love and promised success.

Leader   Glory be to the Creator and to the Christ and to the Holy Spirit.

All   As it was in the beginning, is now, and ever shall be, world without end. Amen.

I Give Thanks for My Ancestors
Psalm in Silence

CALL TO WORSHIP

Leader   May the God who loves justice be with you.

All   And also with you.

Leader   Let us pray this psalm in the silence of our hearts. *(If all do not have a copy, the Leader says: "We open our hearts to this meditation before the face of God present among us and within us." Then the Leader reads it.)*

I give thanks for my ancestors today, Holy God
     present through all history
     keeping all that is in being through all the years of time
Looking back through only-God-knows how many ages
     The chances of *me* ever existing were infinitesimal
Yet elements of me were there
     when the atoms that are in me today were star dust
          or planet parts or asteroid ashes
I give thanks to you, God of History
     and I know my meager thanks is not meager to you
          but is the music you made me for
          and not just music for now but immortal music that is my self

I give thanks for my ancestors
     rejoicing to be the top of a family tree
          whose branches reach back through history
               and disappear down the trunk of nearly endless ages
to the mystery of a seed that found moisture
     and grew nourishing roots in the rich prehistoric soil around it

To be part of such a drama is an honor, Creating God
     a love story, working itself out through all history
          grown now to almost cover our earth
     and a death story as mother earth
          receives each of us back into her re-cycling womb
               wet with the tears of laughter and despair

I give thanks for the honor of being part of it
     I might well not have been

14

And my hope is to carry the colors my ancestors have given me
—and the discoveries and the awe and the humor and endurance—
faithfully toward the future
with faith ever more enlightened
as my life grows on and I myself become an ancestor
of bodies, minds or hearts
flowering into whatever is to come
a future perhaps as rich and expansive as the past

RELATED GOSPEL READING
Matthew 6:25-33 Jesus teaches the disciples to trust in God.

SILENT MEDITATION

Leader   Let us take a few moments to "wait for God," to wait in silence while our Divine Maker sees within us all our needs, our prayers, our thanks, and our communal ties to friends and loved ones. *(After a period of silence, the Leader goes on.)*

JOYS AND CONCERNS

Leader   Open our hearts to each other, Holy God, either through our sharing our own joys and concerns or through our joining in the joys and concerns of others. Make us a community of trust and acceptance. *(Pause.)*

GROUP PRAYER

Leader   We ask you now, Gracious Mystery around and within us, to teach us how to pray, how to speak in our own voices, having reverence for the prayers we feel in our hearts and those we hear from others. *(Pause.)*

CONCLUDING PRAYERS

Leader   O God of our Ancestors, God of all history and of all that is and was, has been and will be, see us here, your children, trapped in time and made for eternity. Give us the faith to be convinced of things unseen, and the trust to hope even beyond hope. As you have cared for us thus far, so we believe you will care for us eternally.

All   Blest be God forever.

Leader   Glory be to the Creator and to the Christ and to the Holy Spirit.

All   As it was in the beginning, is now, and ever shall be, world without end. Amen.

God of Life and Death
Psalm in Silence

CALL TO WORSHIP

Leader The grace of our Lord Jesus Christ and the love of God and the companionship of the Holy Spirit be with you all.

All And also with you.

Leader Let us pray this psalm in the silence of our hearts. *(If all do not have a copy, the Leader says: "We open our hearts to this meditation before the face of God present within us." Then the Leader reads it.)*

Admittedly, Holy Mystery, it is nice to be wanted
> And it is nice to be wanted by you
> It is nice to be wanted. . .
> . . .and that is one way to think about death:

We are wanted
Time is passing each day
> and the little evergreen we planted outside the kitchen door
> now towers innocently over the house

It's an awesome and beautiful thing to look at
> until I realize what it means: time is passing

The little tree now says "Growth-Life-Change
> happens outside your control
> and something other than what you planned is coming about:
> Time."

But does it not intimate also that I am wanted?
> Since it whispers to me of my death
> (my last heartbeat is somewhere on the schedule)
> it whispers to me: I am wanted
> I am wanted at home by Someone who loves me
>> Someone infinite and encompassing in every way
> And wanted by the beloved community yonder. . . .

It is nice to be wanted
> by the God revealed in those who teach us what it is "to be wanted"

It is nice to be wanted by God
> as if by the parents that pro-created us
> as if by the potter who shaped our gifts and limitations
> as if by a creative genius that invented our unrepeatable selves
> as if by a lover who enjoys our nearness and oneness
> as if by a Cosmic Sister God who enjoys with us all our pleasures
> as if by brothers who understand us and accept us

as if by a whole Cloud of Witnesses
who call us home
to be with them yonder. . . .
So we call upon you, God of Life and Death
strengthen us for all our days, including our last,
give us the wisdom to let life have its way
as it brings us to our final hour and moment
Strengthen our faith today
while we have the luxury of peaceful foresight
And while we have the privilege of faith
give us also the courage our life requires
as you have given it to so many millions
of our peers and spiritual siblings worldwide
so we may so pass our days
that our death will be a harmonious part of our earthly life
as well as its end. Amen.

RELATED GOSPEL READING
John 13:31-35 Jesus speaks calmly of his death.

SILENT MEDITATION

Leader In peace of soul, let us silently reflect on life's ending time. (*After a period of silence, the Leader goes on.*)

GROUP PRAYER

Leader Our first prayer request is for the gift of prayer itself. Holy Spirit, hear our simple prayers as we may improvise them now, or to hear our silent prayers acceptable in your sight. (*Pause for prayers.*)

CONCLUDING PRAYERS

Leader May the Holy Spirit of God bless us with unshakeable faith, and give us the enrichment of a community where our sorrows and dreams can be shared. With your help, Gracious Caring Spirit, we can face our future with equanimity, accepting our solidarity with all of humankind.

All Blest be God forever.

Leader Glory be to the Creator and to the Christ and to the Holy Spirit.

All As it was in the beginning, is now, and ever shall be, world without end. Amen.

Praise Our God
from Psalm 33

CALL TO WORSHIP

Leader   May the Spirit of God be with you.

All   And also with you.

Leader   Gracious God, who has made us and this world around us to be such an amazing creation, say the word that will enable us to pray and to praise you in words ever ancient, ever new. Visit us as we believe you can. Make our efforts to speak to you successful today.

All   Blest be God forever.

ANTIPHONAL PSALM
*(Group A—or Leader—reads **bold** lines. The others read regular lines.)*

Praise our God with the sound of the lyre,
> **make melody to heaven with the ten string harp**

Sing to God a new song
> **play skillfully on the strings, with loud singing**

For the word of God is a joy
> **and God's work is done in faithfulness**

By the utterance of God the heavens were made
> and all their wonders by the breath of God's mouth

God gathered together the waters of the sea
> and put the deeps in their trenches

Let the earth revere the Source of Life
> **let all the world stand in awe**

For God spoke, and it all came to be
> **God called out its name, and it stood forth**

Our soul waits for God
> for God is our help and shield

Yes, our heart is glad
> because we trust in the goodness of God

Let your steadfast love, Gracious God, be upon us
> even as we hope in your name

RELATED GOSPEL READING
Matthew 9:35 - 10:8 The vocation of the twelve apostles.

SILENT MEDITATION

Leader　For a few minutes in silence, we ask, Gracious God, that your steadfast love be upon us, even as we hope in your name. *(After a period of silence, the Leader goes on.)*

JOYS AND CONCERNS

Leader　Each of us have a memory full of joys and concerns. This is a moment when those who wish can share those memories—so that our community of faith may become ever more a community of love and shared burdens. *(Pause for joys and concerns.)*

GROUP PRAYER

Leader　Our prayer, first of all, is for the gift of prayer. Holy Spirit, hear our prayers as we may speak them now, or hear our silence, which may be our best prayer. *(Pause for prayers.)*

CONCLUDING PRAYERS

Leader　Dear God, call our names just as Jesus called out the names of his closest companions. We are known to you by name: you knew us before we were born to be named by our parents. And you have your own name for each of us, a name identical with all we are and were meant to be. Call our names so that we may hear them truly, and become, with your help, all we are meant to be.

All　Blest be God forever.

Leader　Glory be to the Creator and to the Christ and to the Holy Spirit.

All　As it was in the beginning, is now, and ever shall be, world without end. Amen.

Sing Praise in the Temple
from Psalm 98

CALL TO WORSHIP

Leader   May the God who loves justice be with you.

All   And also with you.

Leader   Help us pray, Holy Spirit, not only to speak to you—for you know what is in our hearts before we utter the words—but to discover the graces of prayer that come from community. We are often our best selves in the circle of our peers, and learn to pray from the harmony of needs and beliefs and joys and concerns in a context that is wider than solitude.

All   Blest be God forever.

ANTIPHONAL PSALM
*(Group A—or Leader—reads **bold** print. The others read regular print.)*

The ends of the earth all look with awe
    at the wonderful works of God
        Sing praise in the Temple of God on high
            for the wonderful things on earth
        The marvels and mysteries before our eyes
            call for a hymn of praise

The ends of the earth all look with awe
    at the wonderful works of God
        The God of Love wins reverend praise
            from every heart and voice
        Great power flows in creation's art
            so God will ever win praise

The ends of the earth all look with awe
    at the wonderful works of God
        All the ends of the earth have seen
            the wonderful works of God
        Sing joyfully, all you fertile fields
            rejoice in celebration

The ends of the earth all look with awe
at the wonderful works of God
Play on the harp in praise of God
with songs of sweetest sound

With trumpets and strings and drums and horns
sing praise to God with joy
The ends of the earth all look with awe
at the wonderful works of God

RELATED GOSPEL READING
Mark 1:35 Jesus goes out alone in the morning to pray.

SILENT MEDITATION
Leader Let us in silence ask for the grace of "a heart skilled in listening." *(After a period of silence, the Leader goes on.)*

JOYS AND CONCERNS
Leader The joys and concerns of each of us are important to all, for we are a community of faith. Those who care to may take this moment to share with us all your personal joys or concerns. *(Pause.)*

GROUP PRAYER
Leader As you have taught us each to pray silently, teach us, Gracious Divine Presence, how to pray together. As we open our hearts to each other's prayers, we hold up the prayers of all before your loving mystery. *(Pause.)*

CONCLUDING PRAYERS
Leader Holy Spirit within and beyond all that is, we know that your ultimate force is Caring, and your ultimate purpose is the victory of justice and generosity. Fill us with confidence in you today for we know we shall need confidence to face the days of darkness ahead, as we shall also need confidence for our own struggles for justice and generosity.

All Blest be God forever.

Leader Glory be to the Creator and to the Christ and to the Holy Spirit.

All As it was in the beginning, is now, and ever shall be, world without end. Amen.

Save Me, O God
from Psalm 69

CALL TO WORSHIP

Leader May the Spirit of God be with you.

All And also with you.

Leader Be with us, God of our hearts, as together we turn to you in prayer. Our burdens do not feel light, especially when we share the burdens of all our earthly brothers and sisters, young and old, ill or well, safe or in danger. Hear our voices as one voice today, full of faith, thriving in hope, and longing to give you praise.

All Blest be the name of God.

ANTIPHONAL PSALM
*(Group A—or Leader—read **bold** lines. The others read regular lines.)*

Save me, O God
    For I am near drowning
I sink in the quicksand
    where there is no foothold
I have come into waters frightening and deep,
    and the waves sweep over me.
        I am weary with despair
            my throat is parched
            My eyes grow dim with tears
            More in number than the hairs of my head are my enemies
            Those who would destroy me are mighty indeed
O God, you know my folly
    the wrongs I have done are not hidden from you
Let not those who trust in you be put to shame
    O Holy God of multitudes
Let not those who seek you be brought to dishonor
        For it is for your sake that I receive reproach
            that shame now covers my face
        I have become a stranger to my own household
            even an alien to my own
        Zeal for your honor has consumed me,
            and the insults of those who dishonor you—have fallen on me
When I humbled myself with fasting
    it became my reproach

When I made clothing of sackcloth
I became a joke to my enemies
I am the talk of those who sit in the gate
and drunkards sing songs about me
But as for me, my prayer is to you, Holy One.
At an acceptable time, O God,
in the fullness of your steadfast love, answer me
Draw near, rescue my soul,
set me free from all my enemies

RELATED GOSPEL READING
John 19:17-30 Jesus is executed.

SILENT MEDITATION

Leader   Let us enter a period of silence and the mystery at the center of the world's sorrow, pain and faith. *(After a period of silence, the Leader goes on.)*

JOYS AND CONCERNS

Leader   Let us share with each other some of our joys and concerns, for the joys and concerns that we have in our hearts today—and the joys and concerns of our whole world—are uppermost in God's heart as well.

GROUP PRAYER

Leader   Let us gather our thoughts into prayers now, some silent, some spoken—if we wish. May God grant us the gift of prayer all our lives long.

CONCLUDING PRAYERS

Leader   Be with us, dear Spirit of Creation and of Life, as we suffer now in solidarity with all who have had to pass through the trials of death or who draw near to death today. We are not different from them, and fear of death is a natural part of our interior life. Be with us as we seek to be with your son, the Christ, and with all his brothers and sisters in this mortal family. We give you our faith and our trust.

All   Blest be God forever.

Leader   Glory be to the Creator and to the Christ and to the Holy Spirit.

All   As it was in the beginning, is now, and ever shall be, world without end. Amen.

PRAYER OF ANGUISH
How Long, Dear God
from Psalm 13

CALL TO WORSHIP

Leader May the God of infinite compassion be with you.

All And also with you.

Leader We greet you together, Divine Being, Unfathomable Mystery: with your help may we now enter into a time of prayer, when, in this world of distractions and preoccupations, we shall be conscious of your presence— always there in whatever distracts us or preoccupies us, giving all reality its meaning. Without changing to any other, less distreacting, world, let us find you in our own and each others' lives, for we believe that, as we gather to greet you, you come to greet us as well.

All Blest be God forever.

ANTIPHONAL PSALM
*(Group A—or Leader—reads **bold** lines. The others read regular lines.)*

How long, dear God, how long?
 Could it be you are forgetting me?
 Could it be you hide your face from me?
How long must I feel this pain,
 and have sorrow in my heart all the day?
How long shall heart-sickness invade me and rule over me?
 Our own way of the cross is not anything we planned
 We walk on, step after step
  and here we are wondering:
   have we lost the way?
 Or could it be God wants us where we are,
  and asks that we accept the precise future
   as it grows from the present?
Consider, O God, and answer
Give light to my eyes, dear God, my God, lest I sleep the sleep of death
 lest my enemies say, "We have won the victory!"
 lest my foes rejoice because I tremble
 Be with us, Holy One, as our life proceeds and crosses grow heavy
  we put ourselves into your hands
  we do not seek to save our isolated life
   if it means losing our selves.

But I shall have trusted your steadfast love,
and my heart shall rejoice at your rescue
Then I will sing my song to you
because you have been my God
> God of every morning, every sunrise, every warm beam of light
>> be with us in our hopes
>> be with us in our choices
>> be with us in our longing
>>> to come to the light in the presence
>>> and supportive faith of all our friends

RELATED GOSPEL READING
Mark 4:35-41 Mark tells of Jesus calming the sea.

SILENT MEDITATION

Leader   In silence, let us ask, as David did, for the gift of "a heart skilled in listening." Hear the voice of God speaking in the voice of real events as well as in the Scripture. *(After a period of silence, the Leader goes on.)*

JOYS AND CONCERNS

Leader   Each of us have a lifetime of joys and concerns in our hearts, some remembered, many forgotten. Let us open our hearts to one another's remembered joys and concerns, broadening our prayers to include the prayers of us all. *(Pause.)*

GROUP PRAYER

Leader   May our first prayer be for the gift of prayer itself. Holy Spirit, teach us to pray—as you have taught our saints and ancestors.

CONCLUDING PRAYERS

Leader   Dear Unimaginable Creator, Life-force, Center of each thing that is yet beyond us all, calm our fears in the infinity of your being, hear our childish prayers with your heart which is merciful beyond all hearts, and look at our lives as they lie before you, full of anguish, bewilderment—and gratitude.

All   Blest be God forever.

Leader   Glory be to the Creator and to the Christ and to the Holy Spirit.

All   As it was in the beginning, is now, and ever shall be, world without end. Amen.

I Will Guard My Ways
from Psalm 39

CALL TO WORSHIP
Leader   May the Spirit of God be with you.

All   And also with you.

Leader   Before your face and in your presence, Holy God, we come together to pray. Grant that, as you have enabled people to raise their hearts and minds to you over the ages, so today and in this place we shall, with your grace, be able to do the same.

All   Amen.

ANTIPHONAL PSALM
*(Group A—or Leader—reads **bold** lines. The others read regular lines.)*

I am but a passing guest in this place,
     a traveler, like all my forebears

I said to myself, I will guard my ways,
     that I may not fail with my tongue.
I will govern my mouth
     whenever the wicked are present

So I was silent and dumb
     I held my peace—but to no avail
 My distress grew worse
     my heart became hot within me
While I mused, the fire burned

Then I spoke:
     Dear God, let me know my end
          and what is the measure of my days
     let me comprehend how fleeting my life is
Behold, you have made my days very short
     and my lifetime is as nothing in your sight

Surely all of us exist as a mere breath
Surely a human goes about as a shadow
Surely for nothing do we work so hard
     saving up things but knowing not who will gather them in

And now, God, for what do I wait
    My hope is in you alone
Hear my prayer, O God
    and give ear to my cry
Do not remain silent when I weep
      for I am but a passing guest in this place
        a traveler, like all my forebears

RELATED GOSPEL READING
Matthew 16:21-28 Jesus tells the disciples what the future holds for them.

SILENT MEDITATION

Leader Let us take a few minutes in silence to center our hearts on God. *(After a period of silence, the Leader goes on.)*

JOYS AND CONCERNS

Leader We speak of our joys and concerns to each other because we want to be a community—where all are willing to help us with our individual burdens and eager to share in everyone's faith that God stands with us. *(Pause.)*

GROUP PRAYER

Leader Let us pray together, silently or aloud, as we feel called. *(Pause.)*

CONCLUDING PRAYERS

Leader In your good time, Holy God of All, we know there is to be a victory for your love over all the hatred and sin and chaos of this world. We entrust ourselves to your good time, to your way, to your design and providence. Together may we remain faithful and forgiving, energetic and courageous, prudent and unwavering. Your sacred and much-longed-for peace shall come, though the cross is a part of it for us all. Give us solidarity with all who will endure it, and with your son and our prophet, Jesus, who leads the way to life.

All Blest be God forever.

Leader Glory be to the Creator and to the Christ and to the Holy Spirit.

All As it was in the beginning, is now, and ever shall be, world without end. Amen.

May All Who Weep
from Psalm 126

CALL TO WORSHIP

Leader   May the Spirit of God be with you.

All   And also with you.

Leader   We know, Inspirer God, that simply our being in your presence is prayer. And our being together in your holy presence is communal prayer. Our every joy, our every sorrow, our every desire, our every fear—felt in your presence—is prayer. Give us words, Guiding God, if that is your will, or give us silence: we know that is enough.

All   Praised be God forever.

ANTIPHONAL PSALM
*(Group A—or Leader—reads **bold** lines. The others read regular lines.)*

May all who weep in the morning, planting seeds
Come back home singing, rich in flowers and deeds
   Once God rained good fortune on our tribe
      And joy like flowers too thrilling to describe:
      It was a dream! Our mouth filled up with laughter
      We couldn't speak, but only shout thereafter
Then other nations said: *their* God's a wonder
   And we adored our God—
      of flowers and thunder
   Dear God, again rain down good days on us—
   Your desert rain can wash out years of dust
      May we who plant in tears—
         go harvesting with cheers
May all who weep in the morning, planting seeds
Come back home singing, rich in flowers and deeds

RELATED GOSPEL READING
Luke 13:1-35 Jesus grieves over Jerusalem.

SILENT MEDITATION

Leader   In silence, let us ask for the gift of "a heart skilled in listening." *(After a period of silence, the Leader goes on.)*

JOYS AND CONCERNS

Leader Has anyone a personal joy or a concern to share with us all? Our lives can be enriched by solidarity with each other. *(Pause for joys and concerns.)*

GROUP PRAYER

Leader Let us pray for the gift of prayer. Holy Spirit, hear our prayers as we may improvise them now, or hear our silence for that too is our prayer. *(Pause for spontaneous prayers.)*

CONCLUDING PRAYERS

Leader Dear Unimaginable Creator, Life-force, Center of each thing that is and beyond us all, calm our fears in the infinity of your being, hear our childish prayers with your heart which is merciful beyond all hearts, and look at our lives as they lie before you, full of anguish, bewilderment—and gratitude. We are honored to exist in this mysterious world, and we ask perseverance in faith until the day of resurrection.

All Blest be God forever.

Leader Glory be to the Creator and to the Christ and to the Holy Spirit.

All As it was in the beginning, is now, and ever shall be, world without end. Amen.

May All Who Weep in the Morning

from Psalm 126 words and music
by William Cleary

ALL respond.
CANTOR: May all who weep in the morn-ing, plant-ing seeds come back home sing-ing, rich in flowers and deeds.

VERSE ONE (cantor)

CANTOR: Once God rained Good For-tune on our tribe, and joy like flowers too thrill-ing to des – cribe. It was a

dream! Our mouth filled up with laugh-ter! We could-nt speak, but on-ly shout there-af-ter (refrain)

VERSE TWO (cantor)

CANTOR: Then o-ther na-tions said: THEIR God's a won-der! And we a-dored our God of flowers and thun-der. (refrain)

VERSE THREE

CANTOR: Dear God, a-gain rain down good days on us Your de-sert rain can

wash out years of dust! May we who plant in tears go har-vest-ing with cheers! (refrain)

30

You Have Us Mystified
Psalm in Silence

CALL TO WORSHIP

Leader   May God be with you.

All   And also with you.

Leader   Let us pray this psalm in the silence of our hearts. *(If all do not have a copy, the Leader says: "We open our hearts to this meditation before the face of God present within us." Then the Leader reads it.)*

Dear God, you have us mystified
       you enrich our lives with precious persons
              whom we love and care about almost infinitely
       And then you ask us to endure their fragility and temporality
       and often, ultimately, to endure their illnesses, their aging,
              and finally their life's end—
       or, worse, their life's end long before their aging
              the frustration of their dearest dreams and highest promise—
Why, Divine Creator Spirit? Why a world like this?
Why, Holy God of heaven and earth, why the enigma of a world like this?
       Dear God, you have us mystified
       Open our hearts to the gift of understanding
Granted: there may be balancing marvels,
       wonders and ecstasies in our lives
       But it seems that the tilt is so often negative
And many of us never know enough of the bright side
       how mysteriously beautiful are so many of our human race
       how unspeakably dear certain individuals can become
       how glorious can be the natural blossoming of so many living things
       how spectacularly complex, how kaleidoscopic is the microcosm
       how unutterably splendid the sky and cosmos around us
       O unimaginable Source of it all
              you have us mystified

Why is this world the way it seems to be?
       A world that goes on almost as if you are absent
              almost as if you do not hear our cries
We want to ask: Can't Someone do something about *this*:
       this insanity, this injustice, this abuse?
       This dreadful waste of desire, this terrible defeat of promise?

But then someone observes a tender sun
　　　setting over mountains blanketed in mist
Someone discovers that the precious one they love loves *them*
Someone discovers an ocean of caring within themselves
　　　caring without limits or sandbars or shores
　　Or someone is dazzled by a fulfilled family tree
　　　bursting with vitality and endless fertility
　　　and human caring seemingly without limits
　　　　　or any one of a thousand daily miracles
　　　　　that explode into our common human consciousness
And once again it seems that you must exist
　　and be the heart and pinnacle of caring
　　and be a mountain range of colossal mystery
　　and be infinitely and intimately present
　　　even though out of reach of our comprehension
　　Be so for us, Divine Spirit
　　Visit us
　　We know that is within your power. Amen.

RELATED GOSPEL READING
John 12:27-33 Jesus is troubled and in pain.

SILENT MEDITATION

Leader　Let us take a time of silence to enter with Christ into the mystery of pain and uncertainty. *(After a period of silence, the Leader goes on.)*

JOYS AND CONCERNS

Leader　Sharing our ups and downs with others is one way to build community. This is the time for speaking of our joys and concerns—if anyone has something to share with us all. *(Pause.)*

GROUP PRAYER

Leader　Holy Spirit, we know you hear our prayers as we may improvise them now, or hear our silence—for that too is our prayer. *(Pause for prayers.)*

CONCLUDING PRAYERS

Leader　May the Holy Spirit of God give us wisdom and courage for our life's journey, and grant us the enrichment of a community where our experiences can be full of meaning, and our sorrows shared.

All　　Blest be God forever.

Leader　Glory be to the Creator and to the Christ and to the Holy Spirit.

All　　As it was in the beginning, is now, and ever shall be, world without end. Amen.

THE LIGHT OF FAITH
Blessed Are We
from Psalm 65

CALL TO WORSHIP

Leader   May the Spirit of God be with you.

All   And also with you.

Leader   We come to prayer, God of Mystery, with our hearts and minds raised to you, with our enemies forgiven by us, and with our trust in you as strong as we can make it. Empower us now to speak effectively and communally to you as you have taught your psalmists and prophets to do all through the countless ages of time.

All   Blest be the gracious presence of God.

ANTIPHONAL PSALM
*(Group A—or Leader—reads **bold** lines. The others read regular lines.)*

Blessed are we whom you call near
    to dwell in your presence
We shall rest in the goodness of your house
    in the heart of your inmost temple
      You, dear God, make the morning sing
      You make the evening shout for joy

By awesome deeds you answer us and rescue us
    O God of our deliverance
You are the hope of the ends of the earth
    and of even the farthest seas
      You, dear God, make the morning sing
      You make the evening shout for joy

You by your strength have built up the mountains,
    girded with tenderness and might
You can still the roaring of the seas
    quiet the thunder of the waves
    and even the tumult of the nations
      so that those who dwell at earth's farthest bounds
      are awed by your mysteries
      You, dear God, make the morning sing
      You make the evening shout for joy

You visit the earth and water it
　　You greatly enrich it with rain
You provide grain you have prepared:
　　You water its furrows bounteously
　　　　settling its ridges
　　　　softening it with showers
　　　　and blessing its growth
　　You, dear God, make the morning sing
　　You make the evening shout for joy
You crown the year with a harvest:
　　while hills are girded with joy
　　meadows clothe themselves with flocks
　　and the valleys deck themselves with ready grain:
　　　　Together they shout and sing for joy.

RELATED GOSPEL READING
Mark 16:9-16 The risen Jesus appears to his followers.

SILENT MEDITATION

Leader　Let us take time for silence, for listening to the voice of God in our hearts. *(After a period of silence, the Leader goes on.)*

JOYS AND CONCERNS

Leader　Before we turn again to prayer, let us take time for each others joys and concerns—if some feel like sharing them. *(Pause.)*

GROUP PRAYER

Leader　Our most earnest prayer now is for the gift of prayer itself. Holy Spirit, hear our prayers as we turn to you now, or hear our silence for that too is our prayer. *(Pause for prayers.)*

CONCLUDING PRAYERS

Leader　You speak to us, Gracious God, in all real events, in all that is, in all that shall be. We shall belong to your Eternal Household, enjoy the reign of your peace and plenty, and celebrate with all creatures your victory over evil and death. Give us solidarity with each other and with all your vulnerable creatures. Together let us march as one family, believing with all our hearts in the coming success of your greatest desires.

All　Blest be God forever.

Leader　Glory be to the Creator and to the Christ and to the Holy Spirit.

All　As it was in the beginning, is now, and ever shall be, world without end. Amen.

Sing Joyfully to God
from Psalm 66

CALL TO WORSHIP

Leader May the God of all creation be with you.

All And also with you.

Leader Dear God, we long to pray, and we look to you in solidarity with all the women, men and children on the earth. Help us to take our place before you as representatives of them all. For you have made us for yourself, Holy Creator, and our hearts—all of them—are restless until they rest in you. We give thanks that our hearts will find their rest this hour in you.

All Blest be God forever.

ANTIPHONAL PSALM
(Group A—or Leader—reads **bold lines**. The others read regular lines.)

Let all the earth cry out to God with joy
　　Let all the earth cry out to God with joy

Shout joyfully to God, all you on earth
Sing praises to the splendor of God's name
　　Honor the Source of Life through all the earth
　　And say to God: your works win our acclaim

Let all on earth sing praise to you, my God
Sing honor for the wonders of your hands
　　Come see God's awesome wonders on the earth
　　The acts divine inventiveness commands

Let all the earth cry out to God with joy
　　Let all the earth cry out to God with joy

In story God once changed the sea to land
So refugees could cross great streams on foot
　　Therefore let us rejoice in God's great name
　　And in God's hands our dearest fortunes put.
All you who reverence God, come hear me tell
The miracles of wonder everywhere

And blest forever be that Holy One
Who ever sees our needs and hears our prayer.

Let all the earth cry out to God with joy
Let all the earth cry out to God with joy

RELATED GOSPEL READING
Matthew 28:1-10 Jesus appears to Mary Magdalene and the other Mary.

SILENT MEDITATION

Leader We take time now for silent meditation. *(After a period of silence, the Leader goes on.)*

JOYS AND CONCERNS

Leader Let us take a moment to share our lives with one another, believing that each burden we carry or each blessing we receive is a call from God to ourselves and to the community around us. *(Pause.)*

GROUP PRAYER

Leader We have come here to pray, and everything we do here is a prayer, part of our attempt to speak to God in a fully human way. If anyone has a prayer to God aloud or in silence, this is the time for it. *(Pause.)*

CONCLUDING PRAYERS

Leader Dear God of Life, we put no faith in death but live for life and for the life eternal—that life that is in Christ Jesus. In his resurrection and conquest of death we put our faith, and in his victory and success we put our own lives and our own hopes. See us here united in prayer before you, filled with gratitude for your promise of life everlasting.

All Blest be God forever.

Leader Glory be to the Creator and to the Christ and to the Holy Spirit.

All As it was in the beginning, is now, and ever shall be, world without end. Amen.

Spirit Stranger
Psalm of Faith

CALL TO WORSHIP

Leader   May the Spirit of God be with you.

All   And also with you.

Leader   Forgive us, Holy God, for the simplicity of our ways, for the hesitancy of our words. Teach us to pray. We trust that whenever we pray you read our hearts and know our best intentions.

All   Blest be God forever.

ANTIPHONAL PSALM
*(Group A—or Leader—reads **bold** lines. Others read regular lines.)*

Spirit Stranger, are you with us
In this room? Now, really here?
Do you know our names and faces?
All our graces? All our fear?
Spirit Stranger, do you know me?
Do you recognize this voice?
Are my gifts and limitations
Your creations, your good choice?

    Why, Dear Stranger, must you be
    so invisible to Me?
    And so silent, without sound
    warning me that you're around?

        Spirit Mystery, can it be
        you are looking straight at me?
        Though it be naive to do
        I pray someday to look at you!

Spirit! Wisdom! it's beyond me
how you could be really there
And be reading all my feelings!
If you do, what good is prayer?
What's the use of song and worship
if you "know it all" before?
We are taught to sing you praise,
but wouldn't Silence praise you more?

    And, dear Stranger, I'm afraid
    I'm not anything you made.

How could you, who made our sky,
take out time for such as I?
See how potters mold their clay,
washing every flaw away?
I'm so flawed! dear potter-god,
Ah, your taste in pots is odd!
Spirit, may we call you Mother?
Father? Brother? Sister? Friend?
Names all fail! You're wrapped in mystery,
things we'll never comprehend.
So today I'll call you "stranger,"
little knowing why I do,
Knowing Little makes me fear,
but Knowing More is scary too.
Spirit Stranger, this, to me
is your strangest mystery:
How our sorrows you can bear
and not die in your despair!
Spirit Stranger, grant that we
not forever strangers be!
May there come that morning when
we shall see your face! Amen.

RELATED GOSPEL READING
Acts 2:1-4 The Holy Spirit arrives on the first Pentecost.

GROUP PRAYER

Leader   Let us pray as a circle of faith and solidarity. Hear the prayers we each say to you, Holy Creator, either in words or in silence. *(Pause for prayers.)*

CONCLUDING PRAYERS

Leader   Bless our questioning, Divine Spirit, and bless our listening to each other's questioning, for we have found that our questions unite us even better than do our answers. We are searchers together, and while you continue to elude our perceptions, at least we find each other while struggling toward the light.

All   Blest be God forever.

Leader   Glory be to the Creator and to the Christ and to the Holy Spirit.

All   As it was in the beginning, is now, and ever shall be, world without end. Amen.

O God of Otherness
Psalm in Silence

CALL TO WORSHIP

Leader May the God who loves justice be with you.

All And also with you.

Leader Let us pray this psalm in the silence of our hearts. *(If all do not have a copy, the Leader says: "We open our hearts to this meditation before the face of God present among us and within us." Then the Leader reads it.)*

O God of Otherness and Mystery
> **we choose to be with you now in your inner life**
> > **not knowing how to begin to understand**
> > > **the mystery of all you know and witness**
We do know something of the ugliness of pain as you are aware
> **for you were there every time we ourselves experienced pain**
We realize how you suffered all of it with us, and even more than did we
> > **for your love for us is greater than the love we have for ourselves**
And you, poor God
> **inventor of the speed of light**
> > **and of all the distances that light travels over millions of years**
> > **designer/builder of each atom, molecule,**
> > > **life form, species and galaxy**
> > **living outside of time, cosmic mind and heart**
You must witness all the anguish and ugliness of this world
> > **and all through its history and possibly its future**
How profound must be your constant agony
> **for you must be present and witness children frightfully abused**
> > **youngsters recklessly injured and neglected**
> > **young lovers broken-hearted by circumstances**
> > **mothers in doomed childbirth**
> > **fathers torn from their children**
> > **the elderly forgotten and crushed**
all the unspeakable ocean of distress
> > **in each catastrophe, massacre and war,**
> > > **sickness and chance injury**
all the anguish of death, early and late
> > **and of bereavement and loneliness**
and you must witness it all in all its details
> > **yourself somehow unable, like ourselves,**
> > > **to change what's happening**

Gracious God who cannot but empathize with each human sorrow
who suffers therefore whenever we suffer
and rejoices when we rejoice
we condemn along with you the kind of political and military force
that crushed out, so savagely and unjustly
the innocent life of your prophet,
our Lord, Jesus of Nazareth
and we share with you your cosmic grief and anger
at every similar injustice today and throughout history
a sadness growing more heavy with each new outrage on earth
with each unjust killing of a human person
with each innocent person jailed or defamed or abused
or denied a valued role in society or worthy shelter
or a sense of security against hunger and ill health
With your hurt and outraged Presence to help us
we will resist without ceasing, as Jesus did
and with all our strength and resources
whatever is unfair or unjust or destructive of community
and with you we will bless and support the forces of human growth
justice, fairness and unity in our world
We join you in your agony over your creation and are present to you in it
without words or thoughts to comfort you
but only being present as you offer us just your presence
when we are in pain. Amen.

RELATED GOSPEL READING
Luke 13:31-35 Jesus grieves over Jerusalem.

SILENT MEDITATION

Leader   Let us in silence open our hearts to the sorrows of the world. *(After a period of silence, the Leader goes on.)*

GROUP PRAYER

Leader   First we pray for the gift of prayer itself. Holy Spirit, hear our prayers as we may improvise them, or hear our silent hearts. *(Pause for prayers.)*

CONCLUDING PRAYERS

Leader   Speak to us, Holy Spirit; help us to find your loving presence in the events that take place around us, and to resist evil in all its forms while living gratefully in this generous universe.

All   Blest be God forever.

Leader   Glory be to the Creator and to the Christ and to the Holy Spirit.

All   As it was in the beginning, is now, and ever shall be, world without end. Amen.

The Voice of the Spirit
from Psalm 29

CALL TO WORSHIP

Leader   May the Spirit of God be with you.

All   And also with you.

Leader   You are, Holy God, preparing us all our days for prayer, giving each of our concerns meaning, guiding each of our joys toward celebration and gratitude. Be with us at this time of prayer when we reach toward your Infinite Reality and try to imagine and to guess at your Cosmic Beauty and Goodness.

All   Blest be God forever.

ANTIPHONAL PSALM
*(Group A—or Leader—reads **bold** lines. The others read regular lines.)*

Give praise to the Spirit's great power
> **worship our God with awe and reverence**
> The voice of the Spirit is upon the earth's waters
> the God of glory thunders

The voice of the Spirit is awesome
> **the voice of God is full of majesty**
> The voice of the Spirit splits great trees
> God's voice breaks the cedars of Lebanon

It is God who makes Lebanon to skip like a calf
> **and Sirion run like a wild young ox**
> The voice of the Spirit flashes in fire
> The voice of God livens the earth

The cry of God shakes the wilderness
> **our God shakes the wilderness of Kadesh**
> The voice of the Spirit makes the oaks to whirl
> and strips the forests bare

The Spirit of God lives in the waters
> **the Great Spirit sits enthroned in creation**

RELATED GOSPEL READING
John 14:15-21 The true disciple of Jesus keeps his commandments.

SILENT MEDITATION

Leader For a few minutes in silence, ask for the gift of "a heart skilled in listening." We seek the God of Mystery and Presence. (*After a period of silence, the Leader goes on.*)

JOYS AND CONCERNS

Leader As together we turn ourselves toward God, we have in our hearts some measure of joy along with our life's particular burdens. We invite anyone who wishes to speak now of their joys and concerns—so that we may join our hearts in our prayers. (*Pause.*)

GROUP PRAYER

Leader With the grace of God, we can pray together now in this circle of faith and solidarity. Holy Spirit, hear our prayers, or hear our silence for that is prayer as well. (*Pause for prayers.*)

CONCLUDING PRAYERS

Leader We thank you, God of Grace, for the Cosmic Word that was and is Jesus Christ. As he incarnates your Voice and his teachings and example echo your great desires through all ages, let us be also a part of his Body, the very Body of Christ. In all we do, may your Voice be felt, and in all we say, may your Song of Infinite Goodness be heard.

All Blest be God forever.

Leader Glory be to the Creator and to the Christ and to the Holy Spirit.

All As it was in the beginning, is now, and ever shall be, world without end. Amen.

Psalm to the Unknown
Psalm in Silence

CALL TO WORSHIP

Leader   May peace from God and from our Lord Jesus Christ be with you.

All   And also with you.

Leader   Let us pray this psalm in silence. *(If all do not have a copy, the Leader says: "We open our hearts to this meditation before the face of God present among us and within us." Then the Leader reads it.)*

True God, divine Being
      behind and under everything, caring, hiding
            unimaginable Someone
I shine my little spotlight out into your endless, horizonless space
I awaken in the vast deep of your silences
      but conscious of your Being
      a blessing, invisible Presence
I seem like an embryo slowly awakening in the dark
      to a caring, containing, all-enveloping and surrounding Ultimate One
You are my world, my home, my context, my atmosphere, my environment
Here before you I quiet my questions
      silencing my mind, I rest—knowing you, trusting

Of course I have it wrong or mostly wrong,
      thinking of you as a person like those other persons I know:
            who think well of me,
            who support me,
            who care about me,
            who have plans and hopes for me,
            who love me (your creation)
I must have it mostly wrong
      for images do not much help imagine the imageless,
      and analogies can contain falsehoods as well as truth
Still, if you *are*, I believe you must be in some ways like those around me
      made in your image and likeness:
            You think well of me
            You support my efforts
            You care about me
            You have plans and hopes for me
            You love me

So I rest almost wordless and almost imageless
in the darkness of metaphor and analogy
with only my unsuppressible reaching toward you
to connect me and attach me fragilely to you
though knowing you connect powerfully, lovingly, to me
in a torrent of giving and creating.

We are here. It is enough. I give thanks.

RELATED GOSPEL READING
Matthew 18:1–4 Become like little children, Jesus tells his disciples.

SILENT MEDITATION

Leader　For a few minutes of silence, we center our hearts on the mystery within which we live and move and have our being. *(After a period of silence, the Leader goes on.)*

JOYS AND CONCERNS

Leader　Each of us have a wealth of joys and a burden of concerns in our hearts. Let us share our joys and concerns with one another, broadening everyone's prayers, and believing that what happens to each of us is important for the coming reign of God. *(Pause.)*

GROUP PRAYER

Leader　Divine Spirit, hear our simple prayers as we may improvise them now, or hear our prayerful silence. *(Pause for prayers.)*

CONCLUDING PRAYERS

Leader　Our poor prayers together are sufficient, Holy Being, even though they are patently primitive and inarticulate. We have only "unutterable groanings" at times to offer you for prayers: but we know that is enough. You are mystery to our minds but still a natural home for our hearts. So together we journey toward you, giving thanks that we are part of this mysterious world.

All　Blest be God forever.

Leader　Glory be to the Creator and to the Christ and to the Holy Spirit.

All　As it was in the beginning, is now, and ever shall be, world without end. Amen.

God of This Wedding Day
Psalm of Celebration

CALL TO WORSHIP

Leader   May the peace and grace of our Gracious God be with you.

All   And also with you.

ANTIPHONAL PSALM
*(Group A—or Leader—reads **bold** print. The others read regular print.)*

Love's Creator, Love-giving Spirit, around and within us
    help us to weave together the colorful strands of this day
    all its fabrics, rough or silky
        its threads and its yarns
        its cross-stitching, its designs, and its hemming

Weaving Hands, invisible and beyond us
help us make something out of all this:
        the people, the traditions, the memories and the hopes,
        the voices, the faces, the fears and the courage
        the beliefs, the hopes, the affections *and* the chaos—
help us make something, weave something, out of it all

For you, Holy Spirit, wove meaning, it is written, into the Original Chaos
And as much as some of that chaos remains
        on days like this we believe anew in beauty
        and with the help of young lovers
            we taste fresh hope amidst the chaos

and pick up the scent of astonishing promises and of commitment
        startling patterns in the cloth of this despairing world

Weaving Hands, guide our hearts and our minds
        into new and renewed human connections
        as promising as that of our gifted bride and our inventive groom
They are the mystery that fascinated us into coming here
        How we love to look at them! Your work! Your sacrament!

With those Divine Skills that wove this fascinating world into being
        and each of us into its color and excitement
        make us, Holy Mystery, after this day

46

a human fabric that holds together in beauty and in strength
so that the texture of our own lives be enlivened
so that all our connections with each other
like a new marriage for us all
be ever more hardy and more merry

RELATED GOSPEL READING
John 2:1-11 Jesus attends a wedding at Cana.

SILENT MEDITATION

Leader   Let us take a moment for silent centering. *(After a period of silence, the Leader goes on.)*

JOYS AND CONCERNS

Leader   Are there particular joys or concerns anyone would like to share now with the community? We will join our prayers together around them. *(Pause.)*

GROUP PRAYER

Leader   Let us think with gratitude about the blessings of our life, and give thanks with faith and trust that God will be with us through all our future. Personal prayers are now in order, either aloud or in silence. *(Pause for prayers.)*

CONCLUDING PRAYERS

Leader   Holy God who fills hearts, young and old, with human love and affection, give us also the graciousness to have hearts of forgiveness for every human limitation. For we acknowledge that we live in an imperfect world, and that our days are lifted to joy by a lightsome and indulgent spirit. Be with us, All-Compassionate Creator, inspiring us with healing thoughts and hearts large enough for the life we have.

All   Blest be God forever.

Leader   Glory be to the Creator and to the Christ and to the Holy Spirit.

All   As it was in the beginning, is now, and ever shall be, world without end. Amen.

God Shepherds Me
from Psalm 23

CALL TO WORSHIP

Leader   May the Spirit of God be with you.

All   And also with you.

Leader   We are your sheep and you our shepherd and shepherdess. We are your creations and you the Potter who formed us from clay, the Knitting Hands that form the pattern of our lives. Give us the gift of speaking to you today without hesitation. How could you be other than eager for our prayers.

All   Blest be God forever.

ANTIPHONAL PSALM
*(Group A—or Leader—reads **bold** lines. The others read regular lines.)*

God shepherds me
        I shall not want at all
I'm led to find a resting place
        where the grass is green and tall
I'm shepherded to rest
        beside clear water still as glass,
Where my drink is fresh and cold
        and all my thirst shall pass

        Although I roam
                through valleys dark with death
        I have no fear for you are here
                as near as blood and breath
        Your rod, your staff, your step, your silence:
                each will comfort me,
        Good Shepherd! Good Shepherdess!
                You're everything to me.

You cook us food
        and we forget our woes
You rub sweet oil into our hair

> **our wine cup overflows**
> Then feeling full and free to roam
> or sleep beneath the sun
> Your goodness still shepherds us
> until the day is done

RELATED GOSPEL READING
John 13:1-15 Jesus washes the disciples' feet.

SILENT MEDITATION

Leader Let us give a time to concentration and silence, centering and personal prayer. *(After a period of silence, the Leader goes on.)*

JOYS AND CONCERNS

Leader We all have many of the same joys and sorrows—and we pray with gratitude and concern about them. Does anyone have a personal concern or joy to call our attention to—so that our prayers may be more inclusive? *(Pause for joys and concerns.)*

GROUP PRAYER

Leader Our prayer is for the gift of prayer itself, and for all the graces and spiritual enrichments that go with a life of prayer. Holy Spirit, hear our individual prayers as we may say them now, or hear our silence for that contains our prayer as well. *(Pause for prayers.)*

CONCLUDING PRAYERS

Leader Spirit full of love, burning like the sun that makes our life possible and endurable, we are full of gratefulness that you chose us for earthly existence, have cared for us in all our ignorance and need, and have sent us prophets who guide us in the humble ways of wisdom and endurance. See here our thankful hearts before you, lifting up our faces to see in your face an infinite caring presence.

All Blest be God forever.

Leader Glory be to the Creator and to the Christ and to the Holy Spirit.

All As it was in the beginning, is now, and ever shall be, world without end. Amen.

A Lamp Unto My Feet
Psalm in Silence

CALL TO WORSHIP

Leader   May the Spirit of God be with you.

All   And also with you.

Leader   Look upon this group at prayer, Holy Ever-Present God, and see in us the face of your anointed one—for we are the Body of Christ. Together we turn our faces, the Face of Christ, to you. And we know you look upon us with parental affection and unconditional love. Hear our prayers, receive our words, accept our longing.

All   Blest be God forever.

ANTIPHONAL PSALM
*(Group A—or Leader—reads **bold** lines. The others read regular lines.)*

Your saints, Holy God, are a lamp unto my feet
    and a light to my path
The courage and faith of those I admire
    are my meditation all the day
    In your steadfast love
        give me a heart and mind like theirs
    In community with them
        in solidarity with them
            amazing things are always possible
Your hidden holy ones, Guiding God, open my eyes and inspire my mind
    They know the pain of defeat but do not despair
    They feel the rasp of ridicule but do not hate others
    They know heavy burdens but carry on, believing
    Your saints, Holy God, are a lamp unto my feet
        and a light to my path
    The courage and faith of those I admire
        are my meditation all the day
In your steadfast love,
    give me a heart and mind like theirs
In community with them,
    in solidarity with them,
        amazing things are always possible.
    They rise before dawn and cry for help
        They hope in your presence
        Their eyes are awake before the watchmen of the morning

They await your rescue
Your saints, Holy God, are a lamp unto my feet
and a light to my path
The courage and faith of those I admire
are my meditation all the day
In your steadfast love,
give me a heart and mind like theirs
In community with them,
in solidarity with them,
amazing things are always possible.

RELATED GOSPEL READING
Matthew 11:25–30 Jesus prays before his disciples and opens his heart.

SILENT MEDITATION

Leader   In silent meditation, let us be in the presence of the silent God. *(After a period of silence, the Leader goes on.)*

JOYS AND CONCERNS

Leader   Let us take a moment to join in the prayers of each other, and open our hearts to what is in the hearts of each and all. If anyone has a joy or concern to share, this is the time for that. *(Pause.)*

GROUP PRAYER

Leader   Let us express our personal prayers now, reaching out together into the mystery around us. *(Pause for prayers.)*

CONCLUDING PRAYERS

Leader   We cannot thank you enough, Holy Fire of Love at the heart of the universe, for all you have given us, but we thank you particularly now for the human beings in our lives who win our hearts' love and make our days joyful. We give special thanks for our hero and messiah, Jesus of Nazareth, whose humble and approachable ways are an inspiration to us all.

All   Blest be God forever.

Leader   Glory be to the Creator and to the Christ and to the Holy Spirit.

All   As it was in the beginning, is now, and ever shall be, world without end. Amen.

O God, You Are My Refuge
from Psalm 91

CALL TO WORSHIP

Leader   May the Spirit of God be with you.

All   And also with you.

Leader   Holy Spirit of God, teach us to pray—as you taught your prophet, Jesus of Nazareth, at the feet of his parents, Mary and Joseph. As we pray the psalms he knew, may he live in our hearts and minds.

All   Amen.

ANTIPHONAL PSALM
(Group A—or Leader—reads **bold** *lines. The others read regular lines.)*

O God, you are my refuge, they will say
     all who dwell in the shelter of the Most High
     who abide in the shadow of the All Compassionate One
My God, you are my fortress, they will say
     You are the One in whom I trust

          God's strength protects you always from despair
               and under the divine wings you will find refuge
          God's faithfulness is shield and armor
               Never need you suffer all alone

You need not dread the terror of the night
     nor the arrow that flies by day
nor the pestilence that stalks in darkness
     nor the destruction that descends at midday

A thousand may fall at your side
     ten thousand at your right hand
     but ruin will not come near you
You need only look with your eyes
     to see the disgrace of those who despair
But because you have made God your refuge
     the Most High your safe habitation
     no evil shall befall you,
     no scourge be ever near your tent

**For God will give the angels charge of you
to protect you in all your ways
On their hands they will bear you up
lest you dash your foot against a stone**

God says: If someone turns to me in love
    I will deliver them
    I will protect them, because they know my name
When anyone calls to me, I will answer them
    I will be with them in trouble
    I will rescue them from destruction
        and show them grace and honor

RELATED GOSPEL READING
Luke 2:22–40 The Holy Family visits the temple in Jerusalem.

SILENT MEDITATION

Leader   In silence, let us be in the presence of God. *(After a period of silence, the Leader goes on.)*

JOYS AND CONCERNS

Leader   At this time we welcome personal joys and concerns which can enrich the prayers of all. *(Pause.)*

GROUP PRAYER

Leader   Let us pray. Dear God who leads us in our prayer, give us the words to speak to you today. Enrich our minds with gratitude, trust, and petition. *(Pause for prayers.)*

CONCLUDING PRAYERS

Leader   Dear God, Weaver of beauty that surrounds us, Designer/Creator of all children, of all precious loved ones, Inventor of human love in all its power and vulnerability, we give thanks to you for all the energies of love that we know, asking only that you draw us to yourself in everything we love, and sustain us in faith in all of life's dark mysteries.

All   Blest be God forever.

Leader   Glory be to the Creator and to the Christ and to the Holy Spirit.

All   As it was in the beginning, is now, and ever shall be, world without end. Amen.

To Whom Shall We Go?
from Psalm 19

CALL TO WORSHIP

Leader   May the Spirit of God be with you.

All   And also with you.

Leader   We reach into our hearts today to find you, Messiah, Jesus of Nazareth, for you said you would be with us whenever we gather in your name. Be for us the Way, the Truth, and the Life: a Way of astonishing originality and perfect solidarity, a Truth that illuminates our path through the uncertainties of the world, and a Life we are honored to participate in as your disciples, your servants, and your friends.

All   Blest be God forever.

ANTIPHONAL PSALM
*(Group A—or Leader—reads **bold** lines. The others read regular lines.)*

To whom shall we go, O Christ,
you have words of eternal life.
> God's gracious way is a perfect way,
> > a rescuing light to the lost and alone,
> The decree of God is worthy of trust,
> > a guide to all who wander from home.

To whom shall we go, O Christ,
you have words of eternal life..
> The desires of God are good and just,
> > at peace and rejoicing they're aimed,
> The wishes of God will brighten the day
> > giving light where darkness reigned.

To whom shall we go, O Christ,
you have words of eternal life.
> Wisdom begins in reverence for God
> > for to know God's love is a treasure.
> The desires of heaven are truly best
> > and just beyond all measure.

To whom shall we go, O Christ,
you have words of eternal life.
> The love of God is more priceless a good

than a heap of precious gold,
Sweeter that Love than the finest syrup
or the honeycomb's richest lode.
To whom shall we go, O Christ,
you have words of eternal life.

RELATED GOSPEL READING
John 3:13-17 Those who believe shall have eternal life.

GROUP PRAYER

Leader   At this time we share in our personal expressions of prayer—or entrust our prayers to God in silence. *(Pause for prayers.)*

CONCLUDING PRAYERS

Leader   We give thanks, Life-force and Whirlwind of Creativity at the Center of Life, that in your wisdom and generosity you gave our world Jesus of Nazareth. At his invitation and yours, we join our lives with his in the pursuit of the truest Way, the most honest Truth, and the liveliest Life. As did he, we give our lives into your hands.

All   Blest be God forever.

Leader   Glory be to the Creator and to the Christ and to the Holy Spirit.

All   As it was in the beginning, is now, and ever shall be, world without end. Amen.

God of Many Mysteries
Psalm in Silence

CALL TO WORSHIP

Leader   May the God who loves justice be with you.

All   And also with you.

Leader   Let us pray this psalm in the silence of our hearts. (*If all do not have a copy, the Leader says: "We open our hearts to this meditation before the face of God present among us and within us." Then the Leader reads it.*)

God of many names and many mysteries
    are you best named our Almighty *Lord*?
Should we call you mighty
        when you cannot save a daughter in a witch trial?
        (for you would not be God if you could save her and did not)
Should we call you almighty
        when you cannot prevent a child from continual soul-maiming abuse?
when you cannot save a son condemned
                for inconvenient messianic claims
                that put him on the side of the poor
                    and not behind the people in power?
Or would you rather not be called Almighty?

And are you pleased to be called "the Lord" when no other lord
        allows himself to be so insulted and despised—without complaint
Yes, there was a place and a time when "Lord" was the best name for you,
        to establish your primacy above the gods of other tribes
        to establish your primacy above the forces of Evil feared by all
If at one time and in some places
        we humans called you the comforting name "Lord"
        (for it suggests a protecting presence if also a demanding one)
We are aware now that
        that name is no longer comforting for many people
            and no longer our necessary choice
        for that old name means "masculine" and "dominance"
            and we know you are not masculine (nor anything partial)
            nor do you so much dominate as *inhabit* earthly things
                sharing somehow your Being with them

Are you not more a Divine Mother, a Father, even a Sister to us

a Brother, a Lover who pursues us, a ready Friend
a Whirlwind-like Force, a Darkness, a Sunrise

Are you not better named Justice Seeker, World Builder
Miracle Worker, Alma Mater, Home
Light, Warm Welcomer, Heart Healer

Or are you really beyond all names or naming
We listen in silence for an answer

RELATED GOSPEL READING
Mark 14:32–36 Jesus prays to God, using the name "Abba."

SILENT MEDITATION

Leader We add our own inner psalm of silence and gratitude to the prayers of Jesus and of all our human race. *(After a period of silence, the Leader goes on.)*

JOYS AND CONCERNS

Leader At this time we add our personal joys and concerns to the circle of prayer around us. *(Pause for joys and concerns.)*

GROUP PRAYER

Leader Prayer is a gift we ask for whenever we turn toward God. Come, Holy Spirit, and teach us to pray together, in words and in silence. *(Pause.)*

CONCLUDING PRAYERS

Leader May the Holy Spirit of God bless us with a deep caring for all those near and dear to us, and for our Mother Earth and all the creatures that depend upon her. May our Parenting Creator enrich us with a feeling of community with the creation around us, and an authentic sense of responsibility for earth's wellbeing.

All Blest be God forever.

Leader Glory be to the Creator and to the Christ and to the Holy Spirit.

All As it was in the beginning, is now, and ever shall be, world without end. Amen.

The Grace to Shout
A Psalm of Anger

CALL TO WORSHIP

Leader May the God of all be with you.

All And also with you.

Leader At this time, Gracious God, we seek the grace of prayer together. Be with us as we come before you in community.

All Blest be God forever.

ANTIPHONAL PSALM
*(Group A—or Leader—reads **bold** lines. The others read regular lines.)*

We ask the grace today
>**to shout when it hurts**
>>**even though silence is expected of us**
>**and to listen when others shout**
>>**though it be painful to hear**
>**to object, to protest, when we feel, taste, or observe injustice**
>>**believing that even the unjust and arrogant**
>>>**are human nonetheless**
>>>**and therefore worthy of strong efforts to reach them**

Take from us, Guiding God, the heart of despair
>and fill us with courage and understanding

Give us a self that knows very well
>when the moment has come to protest

We ask the grace to be angry
>**when the weakest are the first to be exploited**
>>**and the trapped are squeezed for their meager resources**
>**when the most deserving are the last to thrive**
>>**and the privileged demand more privilege**

We ask for the inspiration to make our voice heard
>when we have something that needs to be said
>>something that rises to our lips despite our shyness

And we ask the grace to listen when the meek finally rise to speak
>and their words are an agony for us

We ask for enough sense of self worth to protest injustice and greed
and enough courage to stand with the meek
though we look ridiculous doing so
for we believe the meek shall possess the earth
though they always seem to be failing

Give us the heart to ask "Why did you strike me"
when we have spoken nothing but the truth
and to join those in danger for a just cause
when we can stand aside no longer
And give us the wisdom to listen whenever the weak can endure no more

May our prayers be a shout when it's time to shout
and our lives be a shout against every injustice
and abuse of what is beautiful, honorable and good

RELATED GOSPEL READING
Matthew 10:24-33 Jesus warns his disciples of rejection.

SILENT MEDITATION

Leader   Come, Holy Spirit, into the silence of our hearts. *(After a period of silence, the Leader goes on.)*

GROUP PRAYER

Leader   Give us, dear God, the blessing of solidarity, both in protest and in prayer. Give us words with which to approach you now so that we may express our prayerful concern for justice and mercy in our world. *(Pause.)*

CONCLUDING PRAYERS

Leader   We ask today, Holy God of Justice, the gift of solidarity with all our earthly brothers and sisters, beginning with those we pray with, stretching then to those we live with, including thereafter our own companions in work and struggle, and reaching especially to the world's most suffering and marginalized. As you care greatly for each, especially the most needy, so may our hearts imitate yours.

All   Blest be God forever.

Leader   Glory be to the Creator and to the Christ and to the Holy Spirit.

All   As it was in the beginning, is now, and ever shall be, world without end. Amen.

Guide Me in Just Ways
from Psalm 25

CALL TO WORSHIP

Leader May the Spirit of God be with you.

All And also with you.

Leader With joy we come together to pray today, dear God of all that is, for we know you have invited us to pray, and have instructed us in the ways of prayer: not to come with fear, not to hesitate to speak, though it be in silence or in only the simplest of words. We acknowledge your presence here, and enjoy this grace of being together along our journey to you.

All Amen.

ANTIPHONAL PSALM
*(Group A—or Leader—reads **bold** lines. The others read regular lines.)*

To you, O God, I lift my soul
I am the creature you made long ago
and I wait in your presence as you bless me.
> Guide me in just ways, O God, My God,
> teach me the paths of honesty and light,
> for your good help I wait all the day long
> Come lead me on and show me what is right.

To you, O God, I lift my soul
I am the creature you made long ago
and I wait in your presence as you bless me.
> Our God is generous to all the crushed,
> And helps the heavy-burdened ones to cope,
> God helps all humble seekers find the truth,
> and shows the poor how they may live in hope.

To you, O God, I lift my soul
I am the creature you made long ago
and I wait in your presence as you bless me.
> The paths of God are steadfast love and faith
> > for those who keep God's covenant and way.
> God's friendship touches all look within
> > and find a path of justice day by day.

60

RELATED GOSPEL READING
Matthew 15:21-28 A Canaanite woman asks Jesus for help and healing.

SILENT MEDITATION

Leader For a few minutes, let us meditate in silence on what we have heard. *(After a period of silence, the Leader goes on.)*

JOYS AND CONCERNS

Leader As we turn to our prayers, has anyone a personal joy or concern that we may include in our prayers before God? *(Pause.)*

GROUP PRAYER

Leader Teach us now to pray, All-merciful God. As we express our prayers in words or in silence, give us the grace of honest, simple prayerfulness. *(Pause.)*

CONCLUDING PRAYERS

Leader We hold in our hearts, All-Compassionate God, all those people we love and all those causes we care about. We know you care about all these things too, and we join our hearts with yours. Share with us some of the peace that you know, seeing all that is from your perspective of infinite wisdom. In union with you, we shall not despair, knowing that with you, all good things are possible.

All Blest be God forever.

Leader Glory be to the Creator and to the Christ and to the Holy Spirit.

All As it was in the beginning, is now, and ever shall be, world without end. Amen.

I Am a Wordless Prayer
Psalm in Silence

CALL TO WORSHIP

Leader   May peace from God and from our Lord Jesus Christ be with you.

All   And also with you.

Leader   Let us pray this psalm in silence. *(If all do not have a copy, the Leader says: "We open our hearts to this meditation before the face of God present among us and within us." Then the Leader reads it.)*

Holy God
> who—in a real sense—does not speak in words
> accept the wordless prayer of my whole self at this moment

Just as all you show of yourself
> (trees, ribboned sky, morning mist, my child asleep)
> speak to me of you and of how you feel about me, about us all

so I AM a wordless prayer before you
> my face, my form, my vital pulses
> my memory and mind, my heart and its desires here
> > all speak to you and in a language you well understand

Here I am, then,
> honored to be with . . ." Thee"
> I . . . Thou . . .

See, I hesitate this moment to use the word "you"
for "you" seem an Other so different from all others I call "you"
> *"Thou* art my God" I once used to say
> but then Messiah called you such a familiar name: "Abba!" "Papa!"
> so I dropped the "Thou" and the "Thee" and the "Thy" and the "Thine"
> and grew familiar with . . . (You?)

But see, today I understand things differently
> how for some religions your name is never even pronounced
> silence and awe is the human instinct

Still at this moment of intimate and thorough communication
> when you wordlessly address me and I wordlessly reply
> I want to describe us as "I" . . . and *"Thou "*

Yet what need is there to address you in a word

when we are so wordlessly in touch?
I hear the birds. I hear the dripping woods, feel a sigh in the wind
You hear my breathing, my heart's beat, the flow of my blood stream
  That's enough sound
There is a We happening
My whole being says a wordless greeting
  and your Whole Being nods and understands . . .

RELATED GOSPEL READING
Mark 1:35 Jesus, long before daybreak, retires to a desert place to pray.

SILENT MEDITATION

Leader In stillness and centeredness, let us put ourselves before the all-knowing God. *(After a period of silence, the Leader goes on.)*

JOYS AND CONCERNS

Leader We would hear now any personal joys or concerns which we may include in our prayerfulness. *(Pause.)*

GROUP PRAYER

Leader Give words to our hearts and our lips, dear God, so that we may be persons of faith. Hear our prayers now both silent and perhaps aloud. *(Pause.)*

CONCLUDING PRAYERS

Leader We trust you, Holy God of time and eternity. Bless us with wisdom, understanding, and patience. Visit us with your grace and your benediction. As you look upon us with compassion, grant us the realization that you are always with us, and will be our eternal companion in the mystery of the life to come.

All Blest be God forever.

Leader Glory be to the Creator and to the Christ and to the Holy Spirit.

All As it was in the beginning, is now, and ever shall be, world without end. Amen.

Your Way Be Done
Psalm in Silence

CALL TO WORSHIP

Leader   May the God who loves justice be with you.

All   And also with you.

Leader   Let us pray this psalm in the silence of our hearts. *(If all do not have a copy, the Leader says: "We open our hearts to this meditation before the face of God present among us and within us." Then the Leader reads it.)*

Divine Spirit,
    Why do you pretend not to be?
    Why does the chaos that often appears to exist all around us
        suggests more a *chaos* in heaven than a *Creator* in heaven?
    When one looks around at the cruel and barbarous things
        men and women do to each other
        to children, to captives, to the trapped and defenseless
        we wonder: where is God? Where are you?
That you could be present at each and every violent scene
    and still not do anything to protect the innocent
        makes it seem like you do not exist at all
    The evil of this world is so great that it seems to blot you out
        make you un-believable
        or at least so preposterously powerless
            that you do not seem like a God
You don't seem to make any effort to seem plausible, Holy Mystery!
    How can a "God" be present at a grotesque injustice
        and not *do* anything?
Why do you pretend not to be, O Source of Life?

The ocean of mystery is, perhaps, far deeper than we had dreamed
    The unknown beyond the horizon of our understanding
        is far more vast than we have imagined
Your "Way" be done. That is easier to say than "your will be done"
    because our word *will* is so full of ambiguities
The way reality is—in the *long* run—let *that* happen
    I can think of it as your way, even if it not be your will
    I can believe there is meaning, even when I don't grasp what it is
What remains for us, as for Job, is faith
    To *keep* faith
    Not to *lose* faith

Not to give in to despair. Not to *curse* the Way the world is
You are with us and in us amide this apparent absurdity
Could it not be that the meaning that stands under all that happens
      especially the pain
      exists—but is simply not humanly comprehensible?
The sightless stars burn, cursing their fate perhaps
      never imagining what they might mean to the cosmos
Like Job, I put my hand over my mouth
      I know that you live
      Let it be. Your way.
      So be it. Amen.

RELATED GOSPEL READING
Mark 15:33-37 Jesus prays a psalm on the cross.

SILENT MEDITATION

Leader In silence let us join our hearts around the great mysteries of life and death. *(After a period of silence, the Leader goes on.)*

JOYS AND CONCERNS

Leader We hear you speak to us, Holy God, in the experience of our lives. Before God, we now share with each other our personal joys and concerns. *(Pause for joys and concerns.)*

GROUP PRAYER

Leader Our prayer is, first, for the gift of prayer itself. Thus may God teach us to pray at this moment, both silently and aloud. *(Pause for prayers.)*

CONCLUDING PRAYERS

Leader May the Holy Spirit bless us with confidence and faith, so we may live within the mysteries of life without despair, and share willingly in the destiny of our race. Give us, gracious God, the enrichment of a community where our sorrows and dreams can be shared, with a hope of an eternal lifetime together.

All Blest be God forever.

Leader Glory be to the Creator and to the Christ and to the Holy Spirit.

All As it was in the beginning, is now, and ever shall be, world without end. Amen.

You Are Mystery
Psalm in Silence

CALL TO WORSHIP

Leader May the God who loves justice be with you.

All And also with you.

Leader Let us pray this psalm in the silence of our hearts. *(If all do not have a copy, the Leader says: "We open our hearts to this meditation before the face of God present among us and within us." Then the Leader reads it.)*

How do the Marsfolk live, Holy God?
Are there "Aliens" who live in the dark?
>   **who like us inhabit a planet, are born, nourished, and die**
>   **but never *see*, never know light**
>>   **light shining on things out of reach, multi-colored,**
>>>   **symbolic, amusing, awesomely beautiful**
>>   **or frighteningly threatening**
>>>   **living by feeling, hearing, smelling and tasting**
>>>   **who never even hear tell of what light is like?**

Or, do "Aliens" somewhere live without air
>   **and the feel and the taste of breathing**
>   **without wind that awakens them and fills up their lungs**
>   **without sound! without talk! without music!**
>   **no scent of flower or tree, no hint of food warming up?**
Are there "people" like that anywhere, Living God
>   **who created our earth and our sea and our sky?**
We cannot imagine them

Yet, Loving Mystery,
>   **do you see as we do?**
>   **have you eyes that depend upon light?**
>   **have you ears that depend upon air, hear music,**
>>   **or listen to words when they're spoken?**
The answer is—No, of course. . .

How can we *imagine* you, then?
>   **We can't**
>   **We know almost nothing about you**
>>   **except that you must exist because we exist**

because we cannot even imagine ourselves
unless there is. . .you

We cannot imagine how you know things without sight or feeling
how you hear without ears
how you mourn
how you know joy
how you care and love
You are Mystery, Holy Otherness
the Unknown Mystery at the center of our lives
whom we long for. . .

RELATED GOSPEL READING
Mark 1:35 Jesus gets up before dawn to pray alone.

SILENT MEDITATION

Leader   Let us take a few minutes for silence. *(After a period of silence, the Leader goes on.)*

JOYS AND CONCERNS

Leader   As we listen now to each other's pressing concerns or recent joyful experiences, we face reality together in the presence of God. *(Pause.)*

GROUP PRAYER

Leader   We turn to you, Holy Mystery, in prayer. Hear us, then, in both our words—if such there be—or in our silent and faithful waiting. *(Pause.)*

CONCLUDING PRAYERS

Leader   Enlighten us, God of Wonders, so that together we may know what you would have us do and say—first here in your presence, and thereafter in each of our lives and in our life together. Give us faith and hope in the darkness of our human intelligences. Carry our hearts through to their arrival at your goodness, support our efforts to blend our inspirations toward the common good. We give thanks, however feebly, for your endless and unlimited generosity to us, Holy Spirit of Light.

All   Blest be God forever.

Leader   Glory be to the Creator and to the Christ and to the Holy Spirit.

All   As it was in the beginning, is now, and ever shall be, world without end. Amen.

Psalm to a MetaBeing
Psalm in Silence

CALL TO WORSHIP
Leader   May the God who loves justice be with you.

All   And also with you.

Leader   Let us pray this psalm in the silence of our hearts. *(If all do not have a copy, the Leader says: "We open our hearts to this meditation before the face of God present among us and within us." Then the Leader reads it.)*

O God to whom we speak so haltingly,
Help us with words to speak of you
    Divine MetaBeing! Divine MetaPerson!
       (where *meta* implies otherness, beyondness) . . .

Some say you are not a *being*
    because the way you exist
        is almost nothing like the way we (and other things) exist
    for there was a time when we did not exist
        but you have existed always,
    and we can conceivably not exist,
        but you can not conceivably not exist;
    and you not so much "exist" as "*are* existence."
    You certainly do not "have existence," the way we (all creatures) do.
So when we call you a being, or say you exist,
    we have to remember you are
        beyond all being we know or can imagine.
So may I call you a MetaBeing? A "beyond being" Being?

Some say you are not a *person*
    since all the other "persons" we know
        have characteristics in their personalities,
        have dimensions to their knowledge and love,
        have traits of mind and heart that we can define
But you must be conceived of as a limitless personage
    with no dimensions, except "infinity," to your knowledge and love
    and no traits of mind and heart except, again, infinity
        in all conceivable qualities
So, since you are beyond all the persons I know or can imagine,
May I call you a MetaPerson?
Whatever you are, you are beyond anything I know:

I know love: that infinite valuation felt for our young or our friends
You are love... in some sense like my love,
some "beyond" sense:
And I know the fierce feeling of overwhelming valuation
for a lover,
and the joy of being loved
But you are love. . . in some sense like my love,
some "beyond" sense:
Whatever you are,
Divine Love, Divine Lover
You are wonder-full beyond all wondering
and beyond all words

RELATED GOSPEL READING
Matthew 7:7-8 Jesus invites the disciples to pray for what they want.

SILENT MEDITATION

Leader Let us pause in silence before the awesome mysteries around and within us. *(After a period of silence, the Leader goes on.)*

JOYS AND CONCERNS

Leader As it is a joy to hear of others' joys, and an honor to share another's burdens, we now welcome our community's joys and concerns. *(Pause.)*

GROUP PRAYER

Leader Whether we speak in silence or in words, we know and believe we are heard by you, Holy Spirit. Give us now the gift of group prayer, perhaps in words, perhaps in silence. *(Pause for prayers.)*

CONCLUDING PRAYERS

Leader Gather up the fragments of our joys and concerns, Holy God, and give them a meaning beyond what we know. We can never appreciate properly how you behold us, just as we can never begin to be thankful enough for your compassionate care.

All Blest be God forever.

Leader Glory be to the Creator and to the Christ and to the Holy Spirit.

All As it was in the beginning, is now, and ever shall be, world without end. Amen.

Lead Us Not Into Illusions
Psalm in Silence

CALL TO WORSHIP

Leader   May the Spirit of God be with you.

All   And also with you.

Leader   Let us pray this psalm in the silence of our hearts. *(If all do not have a copy, the Leader says: "We open our hearts to this meditation before the face of God present among us and within us." Then the Leader reads it.)*

ANTIPHONAL PSALM
(Group A—or Leader—reads **bold** *lines. The others regular lines.)*

Before your face, O Entity full of Mystery
 we come—mystified and bewildered
 victimized by illusions of many kinds
   some we know about but haven't defeated
   some certainly as yet undetected:
 the illusions of immortality, of independence, of superiority
We ask for the grace to look around us today
 with a more growing and searching faith in you
 so that our "faith in you" may give us greater trust in you
   and less trust in our conventional vision of things
 May that greater faith and trust
   draw us toward the mysteries around us
   even to the Heart of all Mystery, yourself, your creating Self
Your communities through the ages
 have often been blinded by illusions
 illusions especially of their rightness and righteousness
   of their divinely guided ability to judge others
    and of their call to point out to others
   the path of rightness and righteousness
 Can you make us honest?
 When we are uncertain, teach us to profess our uncertainty
   rather than give others the illusion
    that we know more than we do
   rather than give others the illusion that **we are divinely guided**
When we have not "knowledge" but only an inkling of something
 let us name the inkling for what it is
   admitting all ambiguity, uncertainty, mystification, and doubt

so that along with our creed we confess also what we don't believe
and what we believe only provisionally, calling on you for guidance
Guide us as we seek out those who can lead us beyond illusion
and who are prophet-like, and prophetic, for us
carrying us past the words to the reality beyond the words,
past the metaphors to the reality beyond the metaphors
to the God who speaks in the voice of real events
to the God who acts in each one's story and history
For we want to know, ever more reverently, your authentic being
not some illusion or distortion of your being
and in the company of the community
to find you where you are: in truth, not in illusion. Amen.

RELATED GOSPEL READING
John 15:4-5 Jesus promises support for everything we do.

SILENT MEDITATION

Leader In silence let us thank God for the "unknowing" that faith brings. (*After a period of silence, the Leader goes on.*)

JOYS AND CONCERNS

Leader Joys and concerns fill our hearts all our lives. In each we hear the call of God. Let us share our experiences of joy or concern—that our hearts may be in solidarity when we pray. (*Pause.*)

GROUP PRAYER

Leader Holy Spirit, hear our words of prayer as we may improvise them now, or hear our silence—for that may be our most eloquent prayer. (*Pause.*)

CONCLUDING PRAYERS

Leader Before your face, Infinitely Wise and Loving Spirit, we rejoice in the mysteries of our faith. In the humility of honest doubt and wonder, we still rely on your grace. And may your presence and blessing be with us always.

All Amen.

Leader Glory be to the Creator and to the Christ and to the Holy Spirit.

All As it was in the beginning, is now, and ever shall be, world without end. Amen.

You Are the Music
from Psalm 92

CALL TO WORSHIP

Leader   May the God of all creation be with you.

All   And also with you.

Leader   Dear God beyond light, illuminate our darkness. Dear God beyor time, be with us during this time that we look toward you togethe Dear God beyond space, walk with us today as we journey together our search for you.

All   Blest be God forever.

ANTIPHONAL PSALM
(Group A—or Leader—reads **bold** *lines. The others read regular lines.)*

It is good to give thanks to God
    to reverence your holy name
    to sing of your love in the morning
    and at night your presence proclaim
    So I play on the lute and lyre
        to rhythm of drum and string
        For you, my God, are the music
        that lives in the songs I sing

For your people will grow like palms
    despite the great heat of day,
And stand like the cedars of Lebanon
    when they lift their branches to pray
    They are strong in old age and grow
        like trees full of sap and green,
    And choose to sing about sunrise
        despite bitter nights they've seen.

RELATED GOSPEL READING
Luke 24:36-53 The risen Jesus leaves a joyful message with his disciples.

SILENT MEDITATION

Leader In silence, ask for the blessing of "a heart skilled in listening." *(After a period of silence, the Leader goes on.)*

JOYS AND CONCERNS

Leader We all feel enriched when we hear of each other's blessings, and we all want to help carry each one's burden. Has anyone a joy or a concern to share? *(Pause for joys and concerns.)*

GROUP PRAYER

Leader We take time now to offer our personal prayers, silent or aloud. *(Pause.)*

CONCLUDING PRAYERS

Leader Holy Spirit within and beyond all that is, we know that your ultimate force is Caring, and your ultimate purpose is the victory of justice and generosity. Fill us with confidence in you today for we know we shall need confidence to face the days of darkness ahead, as we shall also need confidence for our own struggles for justice and generosity.

All Blest be God forever.

Leader Glory be to the Creator and to the Christ and to the Holy Spirit.

All As it was in the beginning, is now, and ever shall be, world without end. Amen.

You Are the Music

from Psalm 92

words and music
by William Cleary

My Rock whose good-ness has no end, You are my God, my Hope, my Friend! My

Rock whose good-ness has no end, You are my God, my Hope, my Friend! (1) It is good to give thanks to
(2) For your peo-ple will grow like

God, to rev'rence your ho-ly name, to sing of your love in the morn - ing, and at
palms, des-pite the great heat of day, and stand like the ce - dars of Le-be - non when they

night your pre-sence pro-claim. So I play on the lute and lyre to rhy-thm of drum and
stretch their branches to pray, They are strong in old age, and grow like trees full of sap and

string, for You, dear God, are the mu - sic that lives in the song I sing.
green, and choose to sing a - bout sun-rise des-pite bit-ter nights they've seen.

How Majestic Is Your Name
from Psalm 8

CALL TO WORSHIP

Leader   May the Spirit of God be with you.

All   And also with you.

Leader   Holy Spirit of God, teach us to pray—as you taught your prophet and our humble Lord, Jesus of Nazareth, at the feet of his parents, Mary and Joseph. As we pray the psalms he knew, may he live in our hearts and minds.

All   Amen.

ANTIPHONAL PSALM
*(Group A—or Leader—reads **bold** print. The others read regular print.)*

O God of Every Mystery
how majestic is your name in all the earth
     You whose honor is higher than the sky
     Your praise is chanted by the mouths of babies and of infants
You dwell within and around us
     and we stand beyond the reach of any enemy
     When I look at the heavens, the work of your fingers
          the moon and the stars which you have established
          what is humankind that you are mindful of us
          what are earthlings that you can care for us
Yet you have made us almost divine
     and crown us with laughter and glory
     You have given us responsibility for the works of your hands
     You have put all things into our care:
          all sheep and oxen, and also the beasts of the field
          the birds of the air, and the fish of the sea
     and whatever passes along the underwater paths of the ocean.
O God of Every Mystery
     how majestic is your name in all the earth

RELATED GOSPEL READING
Luke 1:39-55 Mary greets Elizabeth with a song of thanks and liberation.

SILENT MEDITATION

Leader We add to Mary's canticle our own inner psalm of silence and gratitude. *(After a period of silence, the Leader goes on.)*

JOYS AND CONCERNS

Leader Let us take a moment now to share our personal joys and cares. *(Pause.)*

GROUP PRAYER

Leader Has anyone a personal prayer to offer? We take time now for all our prayers, both silent and aloud. *(Pause for prayers.)*

CONCLUDING PRAYERS

Leader May the Holy Spirit of God bless us with a deep caring for all those near and dear to us, and for our Mother Earth and all the creatures that depend upon her. May our Parenting Creator enrich us with a feeling of community with the creation around us, and a authentic sense of responsibility for earth's well-being.

All Blest be God forever.

Leader Glory be to the Creator and to the Christ and to the Holy Spirit.

All As it was in the beginning, is now, and ever shall be, world without end. Amen.

A Psalm About Competition
Psalm in Silence

CALL TO WORSHIP

Leader   May the God who loves justice be with you.

All   And also with you.

Leader   Let us pray first in the silence of our hearts. *(If all do not have a copy, the Leader says: "We open our hearts to this meditation." Then the Leader reads it.)*

Spirit of Life
    Inventor/Parent
    of each unique man and woman,
Help me keep in balance my good self-esteem
        for qualities not really comparable to others'
        (I'm imcomparable!)
    despite the unbalancing momentum of competitiveness
      that would carry me toward clownishly looking down on others
        or fretfully looking up at their supposed superiority
They are not really worse or better,
    they are *just like* . . . me
And I am your child/creation and so are they
They are, each of them, your gift to me
    brothers and sisters to be respected and listened to,
    then spoken to honorably and respectfully
        without condescension or fear
          for I am also your gift and blessing to them

Is there anyone on earth who cannot say:
    "I am in many ways blessed"?
I don't know
Certainly I have to say it.
I am blessed in my being and all that goes with it
    my heartbeat
    my thoughts
    my memories
    my ties with others
blessed with the inspiration of people
    who endure hardship bravely
blessed with those who look at me with caring
blessed with my future, however you and I will shape it

So I ask only to belong to the human race this moment and this day
to be human in spirit as well as in reality
to be one of the humans who look to you with awe and gratitude.
I reject all my infantile inclinations
to envy those to appear luckier than myself
I laugh at my clownish mind-habits of comparison living
Let me be moldable clay in your hands, Potter God
listening to your voice in real events
useful to my fellow creatures, to my communitites
and to our mother earth
and seeking only the first prize
for Ourstanding and Fearless Myself-hood

RELATED GOSPEL READING
Matthew 6:1-6 Jesus gives advice to his disciples.

SILENT MEDITATION

Leader We center our hearts in silent meditation. *(After a period of silence, the Leader goes on.)*

JOYS AND CONCERNS

Leader Let us take a moment to welcome joys and concerns from anyone here so that we may add them to our personal and communal prayers. *(Pause.)*

GROUP PRAYER

Leader If prayers come to our lips, let us say them now; if prayers are in our hearts, let us raise them up before our divine Creator. *(Pause.)*

CONCLUDING PRAYERS

Leader You know our hearts, dear God of the Universe. You see our past as plainly as the present, and see all our inner potential as well as our most obvious strengths. We give thanks that we know you and feel your presence in all creation, confident that in life's mysteries there is the same glowing meaning that we already find everywhere.

All Blest be God forever.

Leader Glory be to the Creator and to the Christ and to the Holy Spirit.

All As it was in the beginning, is now, and ever shall be, world without end. Amen.

Index

Psalm Services for Particular Times

Psalms for Liturgical Seasons

Numerical List of Scriptural Psalms

Alphabetical List of Poetic Titles

✤ *Of Related Interest...*

Psalm Services for Parish Meetings
William Cleary

Nearly 40 separate services based on themes such as peace and justice, caring for Earth, forgiveness, appreciation and hope.
ISBN: 0-89622-473-2, 80 pp, $9.95

Prayer Services for Parish Meetings
Debra Hintz

These 40 Scripture-based prayer services can be used to open and close a variety of meetings in the parish.
ISBN: 0-89622-170-9, 96 pp, $9.95

Gathering Prayers
Debra Hintz

The emphasis of the book is on the seasons, topics of broadly ecumenical interest and concern and a variety of themes on praise and thanksgiving.
ISBN: 0-89622-296-9, 80 pp, $9.95

Available at religious bookstores or from
TWENTY-THIRD PUBLICATIONS
P.O. Box 180 • Mystic, CT 06355
1-800-321-0411